GARLINGHOUSE

Single-Level Home Plans
With Special Underground and Berm Designs

Contents

You'll Enjoy Peace and Quiet

No. 25002

The excellent design of the floor plan buffers living and sleeping areas with stairway, master bath, closets, and a hall. The bedrooms are clustered together, yet non shares a wall with another or with the living room. The family playroom is downstairs along with a bedroom, bath, laundry, storage. A large fireplace wall in the living room and dining room create a feeling of warmth, while the cathedral ceiling with dark contrasting beams gives a sense of spaciousness.

Main level — 2,263 sq. ft.
Lower level — 1,290 sq. ft.
Garage — 528 sq. ft.

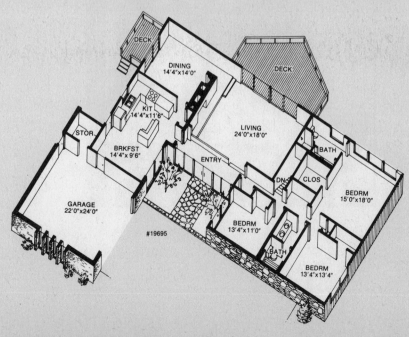

Charming Three-Bedroom Rancher

No. 26741

This charming home features something for everyone, the romantic, the outdoor enthusiast or the traditionalist. A sunken living room provides a lovely conversation area with a beautiful view of the great outdoors. An energy saving fireplace in the family room provides not only heat but a cozy atmosphere for those family gatherings. A well designed kitchen and dining room provides ease of entertaining, both casual and formal. Grouped separate from the living areas are the bedrooms, the large master bedroom shows a dressing room and private full bath while two junior bedrooms share a centrally located bath. A hot tub highlights the large deck area accessible from either the family room or the master bedroom. A laundry links the garage with the kitchen.

Living area — 1,657 sq. ft. (excluding garage and deck)

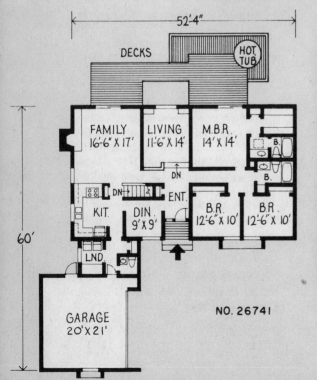

DECKS

HOT TUB

| FAMILY 16'-6" X 17' | LIVING 11'-6" X 14' | M.B.R. 14' X 14' | B. |
| | DN | | B. |

KIT.

DN

ENT.

DIN 9' X 9'

B.R. 12'-6" X 10'

B.R. 12'-6" X 10'

LND.

GARAGE 20' X 21'

52'-4"

60'

NO. 26741

Practical and Energy-Conscious Four-Bedroom Ranch

No. 26780

A low-maintenance exterior of fir siding with cedar battens which will grow more beautiful with age, and the energy-saving Plen-wood heating and air-conditioning system make this one-level house a very desirable choice. One enters by crossing a pine deck with trellis rafters and then passing into a separate foyer. A large living room lies directly behind the foyer, distinguished by clerestory windows flanking a stone fireplace, and rear sliding glass doors opening to a screened porch.

First floor — 2,500 sq. ft.
Screened porch — 238 sq. ft.
Wood deck — 349 sq. ft.
Garage — 614 sq. ft.

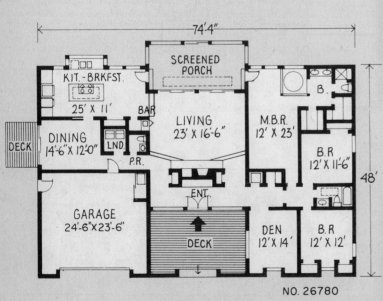

KIT.-BRKFST.
25' X 11'

DINING
14'-6" X 12'-0"

DECK

GARAGE
24'-6"X23'-6"

BAR

LND.

P.R.

SCREENED
PORCH

LIVING
23' X 16'-6"

ENT.

DECK

M.B.R.
12' X 23'

B.

B. R
12' X 11'-6"

DEN
12' X 14'

B. R
12' X 12'

74'-4"

48'

NO. 26780

Energy Efficient Plan Uses Berms

No. 10358

Semi-underground to save energy, this handsome design calls for soil bermed up to the cornices on sides and back and an airlock type vestibule. Plenty of warm sunlight penetrates the well-windowed front, designed to face south, and rear and side window wells allow for emergency exits. For family-oriented livability, the great room with wood-burning fireplace merges with the dining area, and a functional corridor kitchen is handy to both. Located off the double garage, the mud room functions as a laundry and utility area. Three large bedrooms share two full baths.

First floor — 1,620 sq. ft.
Garage — 488 sq. ft.

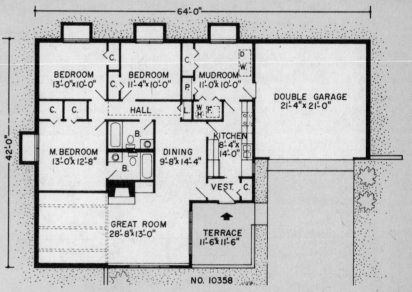

SOLAR HOME

Underground Delight

No. 10376

This three bedroom, underground masterpiece is designed to fight the high cost of living through its many energy saving features, including the use of passive solar energy. The large master bedroom on one end shows an abundance of closets. Each of the three bedrooms has sliding glass doors to the front lawn. Also featured in this area is a multi-purpose room, easily converted to individual use, graciously separated from the entry way by ornately carved wood room dividers. The plan calls for 2 baths, one delightfully designed with a whirlpool. The family room opens to a greenhouse via sliding glass doors. A two car garage completes this home.

2,086 sq. ft.

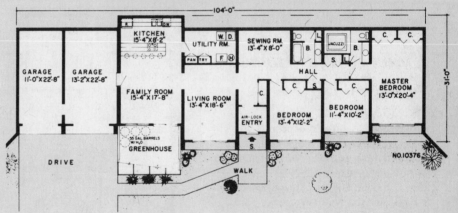

SOLAR HOME

Underground Home Cuts Energy Use

No. 10364

Oriented to a southern exposure, this underground home combines all the comforts of a well-planned contemporary with a fraction of the typical energy consumption. The pre-stressed concrete roof is covered with two feet of earth, a highly effective insulator, to keep winter cold out, warmth in. Walls on three sides are of 8-inch poured concrete. In addition to this functional approach, the plan is highly livable . . . with a protected patio reached by sliding glass doors and an immense open living area featuring family room, living room, and kitchen with snack bar. Bedrooms are large, and the master bedroom annexes a private bath and three closets.

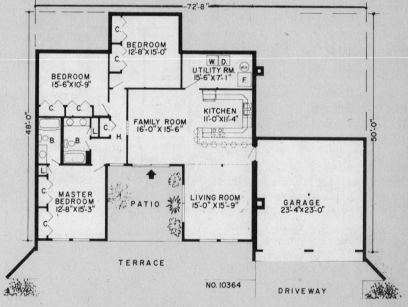

SOLAR HOME

8

Glass Walls
Seem to Enlarge
Front Living Areas

No. 10482

The second floor of this original design contains two bedrooms plus a shared walk-through bath. Fronting the second floor are the stairway and a balcony which overlooks the glass-walled living room. The dining room also boasts a front glass wall and opens onto the efficient U-shaped kitchen. The full bath on the first floor may be accessed privately through the master bedroom or off the central hall. The laundry room, which also includes the utility area, is conveniently located between the kitchen and the master bedroom.

First floor — 966 sq. ft.
Second floor — 455 sq. ft.
Garage — 355 sq. ft.

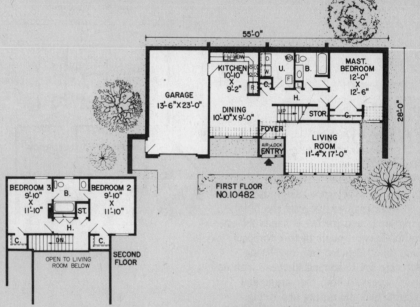

FIRST FLOOR
NO. 10482

SOLAR
HOME

Berm Design Combines Good Looks with Energy Efficiency

No. 10498

Warmed by earthen walls on three sides, this simple yet elegant design uses an open floor plan to integrate the family living areas and further enhance the energy efficient aspects of this compact home plan. Blended into one living space are the U-shaped kitchen, with its direct access to both the garage and laundry, plus the dining and living rooms. A hearthed fireplace plus built-in bookcases highlight these living areas. A short hall leads to the three bedrooms, each with a south-facing window for additional passive solar gain. Two baths and spacious closets complete the sleeping quarters of this compact design.

Living area — 1,419 sq. ft.
Garage — 476 sq. ft.

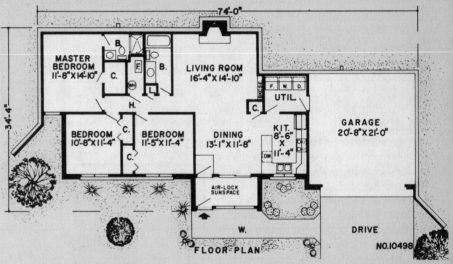

FLOOR PLAN

SOLAR HOME

Energy Savings and Beauty

No. 26050

An unbeatable combination. This passive solar underground two bedroom home offers the unique ability of combining two energy saving features with beauty, grace and style. Highlighting this home is a sunken courtyard and an attached greenhouse/sunroom, for that summer feeling in the winter. The foliage also keeps the climate in this well sealed home fresh. A skylight floods the spacious kitchen with sunlight and a central fireplace separates the living room from the family/dining area, allowing for an open spacious feeling. A study and well designed utility room completes this excellently zoned floor plan.

1,934 sq. ft.

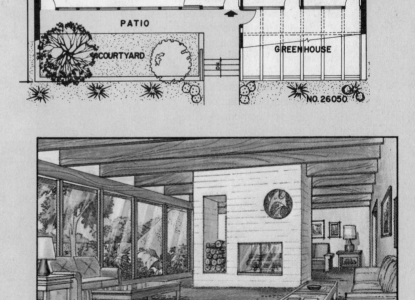

GUEST RM. OR STUDY 11'-2"x12'-6"
SP. WS. H.W.
UTIL.
KITCHEN 11'-4"x12'-6"
65'-0"
46'-0"
LIVING ROOM 14'-0"x18'-0"
FP. WOOD
FAMILY/DINING 14'-4"x18'-0"
H.
C.
C.
B.
BEDROOM 11'-6"x12'-2"
BEDROOM 11'-3"x14'-6"
ENTRY
PATIO
COURTYARD
GREENHOUSE
DN.
NO. 26050

SOLAR HOME

Underground with Greenhouse

No. 26600

This quality home shows many delightful features designed to conserve energy and provide lots of enjoyment. The thoughtfully planned kitchen and the spacious living/dining room combination are centrally located with sliding glass doors opening to the large greenhouse complete with sauna. A large bedroom on each end provides plenty of privacy and both have sliding glass doors, one exiting to the greenhouse and the other to the patio. Storage space abounds in this lovely underground home.

**First floor — 1,609 sq. ft.
Greenhouse — 910 sq. ft.**

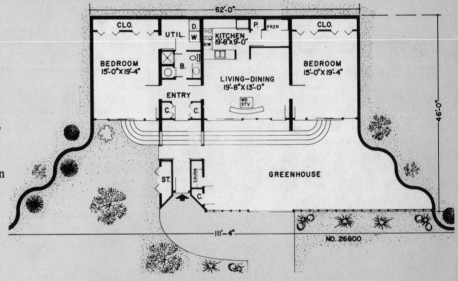

SOLAR HOME

Fight the High Cost Of Energy

No. 26601

This striking contemporary passive solar home, designed for a growing family, can help combat run-away fuel bills. Large expanses of glass on the south side warms the house during the day while storing heat in solar water tubes positioned behind windows for heat at night. Master bedroom has private bath and a redwood deck. Living room, dining room and kitchen are the central attractions in this well zoned home. Sliding glass doors give access to the patio from both the living room and dining room. Two bedrooms share a patio accessible from each room via sliding glass doors. The north side of the house is bermed up with earth for protection from cold north winds. Super insulation in walls and ceiling complete this energy efficient, economical home.

1,748 sq. ft.

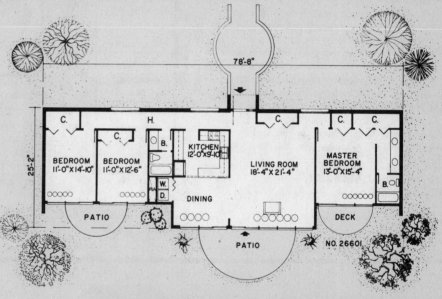

78'-8"

25'-2"

| BEDROOM 11'-0" X 14'-10" | BEDROOM 11'-0" X 12'-6" |
| C. | C. |

H.
B.
KITCHEN 12'-0" X 9'-10"
W. D.
DINING
LIVING ROOM 18'-4" X 21'-4"
C.
MASTER BEDROOM 13'-0" X 15'-4"
C.   C.
B.

PATIO

PATIO

DECK

NO. 26601

SOLAR HOME

Fireplace In Living And Family Room

No. 9263

This beautiful Ranch design features an extra large living room with plenty of formal dining space at the end. A large wood-burning fireplace is found in both the living room and the family room. The busy housewife will appreciate the mud area. It contains the laundry equipment, a half bath and a large storage closet or pantry. Notice how the bedroom area is zoned away from the rest of the house, thereby providing maximum privacy and quiet. Since the house is basementless, a large storage room behind the garage is provided.

First floor-1,878 sq. ft.
Garage-538 sq. ft.

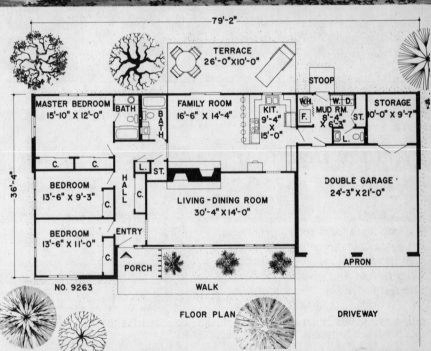

Fireplace A Feature

No. 9838

Family convenience is emphasized in this beautiful ranch style home. The owner's suite includes double closets and a private bath with a spacious built-in vanity. A two-way wood-burning fireplace between the living room and dining room permits the fire to be enjoyed from both rooms. An extra large garage possesses an abundance of extra storage space.

First floor-1,770 sq. ft.
Basement-1,770 sq. ft.
Garage-700 sq. ft.

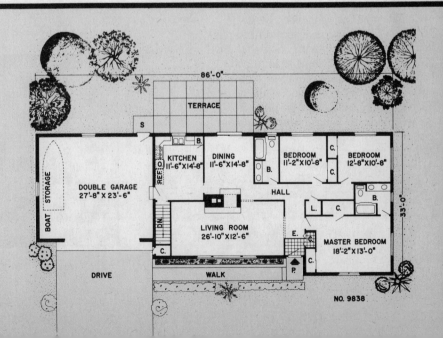

Trim Plan Designed For Handicapped

No. 10360

Attractive and accessible, this three bedroom home has been carefully detailed to provide both comfort and self-sufficiency for the handicapped individual. Ramps allow entry to garage, patio and porch. Doors and windows are located so that they can be opened with ease, and both baths feature wall-hung toilets at a special 16-18'' height. Spacious rooms, wide halls, and the over-sized double garage allows a wheelchair to be maneuvered with minimal effort, and the sink and cooktop are also located with this in mind. Besides these functional aspects, the design also boasts a great room.

First floor-1,882 sq. ft.
Garage-728 sq. ft.

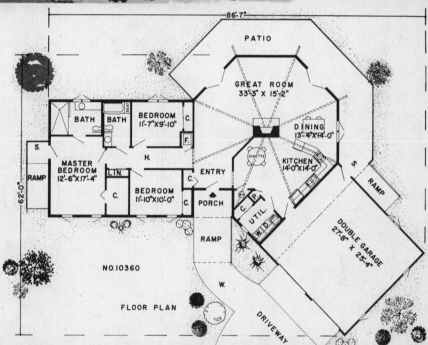

FLOOR PLAN

- PATIO
- GREAT ROOM 33'-3" X 15'-2"
- DINING 13'-4"X14'-0"
- KITCHEN 14'-0"X14'-0"
- BATH
- BATH
- BEDROOM 11'-7"X9'-10"
- MASTER BEDROOM 12'-6"X17'-4"
- BEDROOM 11'-10"X10'-0"
- ENTRY
- PORCH
- RAMP
- UTIL.
- W.I.D.
- DOUBLE GARAGE 27'-8" X 25'-4"
- DRIVEWAY
- RAMP
- 86'-7"
- 62'-0"
- NO.10360

Semicircular Terrace Offers Access

No. 9882

Spanning four rooms to the rear of the home, the semi-circular terrace in this plan is accessible through sliding glass doors from the living room, dining room and family room. The sunken living room with fireplace borders the formal dining room, and a kitchen with laundry space is situated to serve both dining room and family room. Three of the bedrooms, including the master bedroom which merits a bath and large closet, face front and enjoy lovely bay windows.

First floor-2,212 sq. ft.
Basement-2,212 sq. ft.
Garage-491 sq. ft.

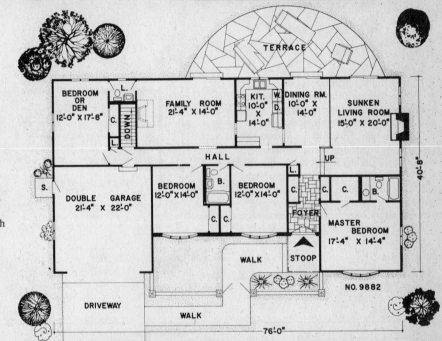

Fireplace Inspires Romantic Dining

No. 9908

Pleasurable dining in the expansive living-dining area is created by the atmospheric woodburning fireplace in this brick-layered traditional. A functional breakfast bar joins the kitchen and family room, which is placed to enjoy the terrace. A gracious foyer eliminates cross-traffic and allows access to the living or sleeping wing, where three sizable bedrooms and two full baths are provided. The double garage also opens to the terrace.

First floor-1,896 sq. ft.
Basement-1,896 sq. ft.
Garage-509 sq. ft.

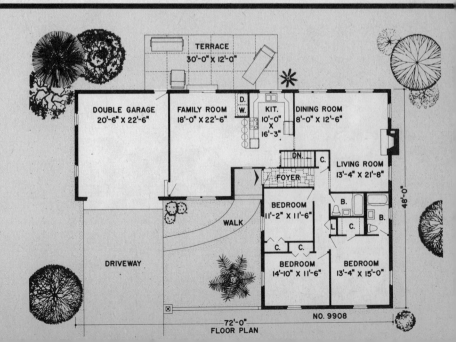

Living Room Expresses Warmth, Formality

No. 10088

Set to the left of the tiled foyer and adjoining a formal dining room, the living room of this trim ranch style offers an expansive area for entertaining and relaxing before a warm wood fire. Connected to the dining room via sliding glass doors is a large dining porch that encourages cookouts and informal parties. Family activity is centered in the kitchen/family room, with sliding glass doors connecting it to the rear patio. Three bedrooms include a luxurious master bedroom with walk-in closet and private bath.

First floor-1,655 sq. ft.
Basement-1,655 sq. ft.
Garage-535 sq. ft.

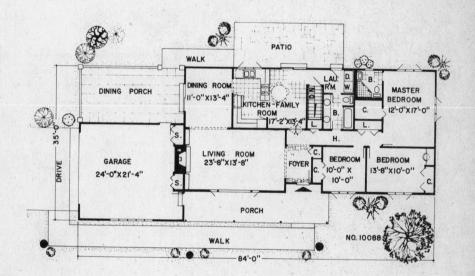

Cupolas and Ornamental Iron Add Prestige

No. 9944

A home like this one retains its resale value indefinitely. The stone veneer construction provides a low maintenance exterior and is extremely attractive. The floor plan features three large bedrooms plus a den, two full baths, a powder room near the front entrance and a half bath near the den and laundry. The centrally located kitchen opens into the family room. A breakfast bar divides the two rooms. The family room has a wood burning fireplace.

First floor — 2,422 sq. ft.
Basement — 2,422 sq. ft.
Garage — 533 sq. ft.

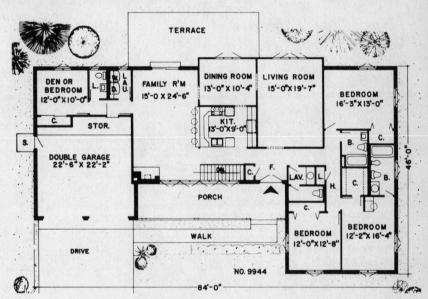

Hexagonal Living Room Elevates Design

No. 9954

Soaring above the main body of the home, the hexagonal living room captures the startling uniqueness of this design. The sunken living room comes alive with firelight and clerestory windows, and with the formal dining room, enjoys sliding glass doors to the terrace. The sizable kitchen apportions laundry and eating space, and adjoins the family room. Four ample bedrooms and two full baths comprise the sleeping wing, which include a family bath with tub and shower stall.

First floor-2,210 sq. ft.
Basement-754 sq. ft.
Garage-576 sq. ft.

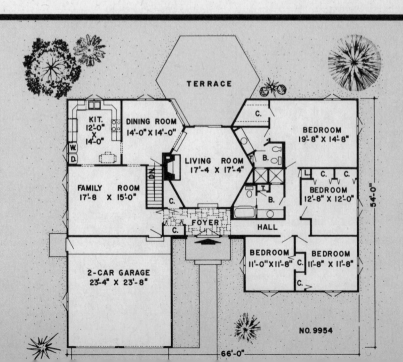

18

Cupola Crowns
Well-Placed Garage

No. 9866

Trimmed with shutters, diamond light windows, and a cupola, the garage of this charming traditional exemplifies the successful fusion of appeal and convenience. The garage opens to the combination laundry and mud room opposite the kitchen. A spacious firelit family room opens to the terrace, where a built-in barbecue grill simplifies outdoor cooking. Three sizable bedrooms flank the formal living room and include a master bedroom with bath and double closets. A covered porch shades the front entrance.

First floor — 1,768 sq. ft.
Basement — 1,768 sq. ft.
Garage — 528 sq. ft.

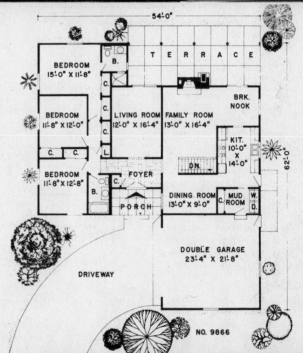

54'-0"

BEDROOM 15'-0" X 11'-8"
B.
TERRACE
BRK. NOOK

BEDROOM 11'-8" X 12'-0"
LIVING ROOM 12'-0" X 16'-4"
FAMILY ROOM 13'-0" X 16'-4"
KIT. 10'-0" X 14'-0"

62'-0"

BEDROOM 11'-8" X 12'-8"
B.
FOYER
DN.

PORCH
DINING ROOM 13'-0" X 9'-0"
MUD ROOM
W. D.

DRIVEWAY

DOUBLE GARAGE 23'-4" X 21'-8"

NO. 9866

Come On In, The Living's Fine

No. 9828

This house leaves little to be desired in a comfortable family home. A few of the most outstanding features are a private patio off of the master bedroom; a two-way fireplace between the living room and family room; a built-in charcoal grill in the family room; a bath with shower next to the kitchen and handy to the pool area and a very nice breakfast nook with a view of the pool area. The mud room is large enough to serve as a sewing and ironing room as well as the laundry. The low maintenance exterior of beautiful natural stone blends well with the shake shingle roof.

First floor – 2,679 sq. ft.
Basement – 2,679 sq. ft.
Garage – 541 sq. ft.

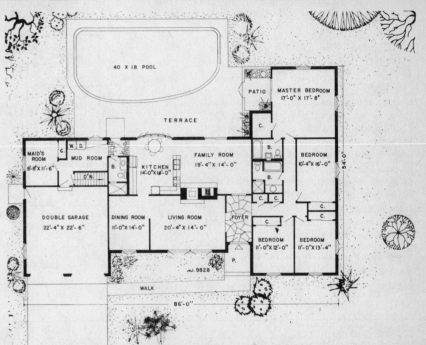

U-shaped Floor Plan Organizes Home Into Living Zones

No. 10450

The family area of this home begins at the back with the spacious family room and moves forward into the tiled in-kitchen eating area with its built-in hutch. Marking the boundary of the triangular kitchen is a serving counter which contains only a few of the many cabinets incorporated into this functional design. The formal dining room is located to the front of the kitchen for easy access. Centrally placed within the home is the beamed-ceiling living room that looks onto the patio and is accented by a bookcase-flanked fireplace. The sleeping zone is made up of two spacious bedrooms plus a master suite.

First floor-2,143 sq. ft.
Garage-465 sq. ft.

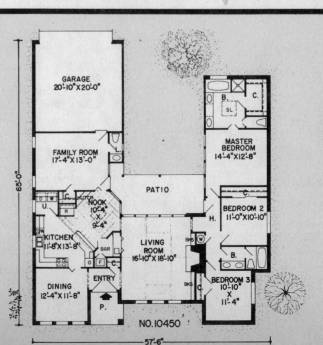

Brick-layered Home
Plans 4 Bedrooms

No. 22004

Four roomy bedrooms, featuring a master bedroom with extra large bath, equip this plan for a large family or overnight guests. The centrally located family room merits a fireplace, wet bar, and access to the patio, and a dining room is provided for formal entertaining. An interesting kitchen and nook, as well as two and one half baths, are featured.

House-2,070 sq. ft.
Garage-474 sq. ft.

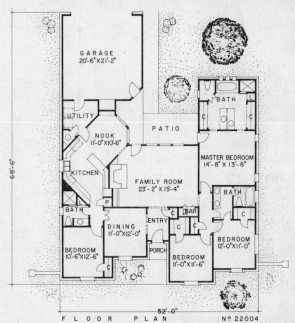

GARAGE
20'-6" X 21'-2"

UTILITY

NOOK
11'-0" X 10'-6"

PATIO

BATH

MASTER BEDROOM
14'-8" X 13'-8"

KITCHEN

FAMILY ROOM
23'-2" X 15'-4"

BATH

BATH

DINING
11'-0" X 12'-0"

ENTRY

BAR

BEDROOM
10'-6" X 12'-6"

PORCH

BEDROOM
11'-0" X 11'-6"

BEDROOM
12'-0" X 11'-0"

68'-6"

52'-0"

FLOOR PLAN   N° 22004

Rustic Ranch Integrates Outdoors

No. 10142

Appendaging a 31-foot redwood deck at rear and a long front porch, this ranch plan offers a woodsy appeal and plenty of involvement with the outdoors. Inside, the floor plan caters to the relaxed lifestyle of the seventies. Flanking the large foyer is the spacious sunken living room, warmed by a wood-burning fireplace.

First floor—1,705 sq. ft.
Basement—1,705 sq. ft.
Garage—576 sq. ft.

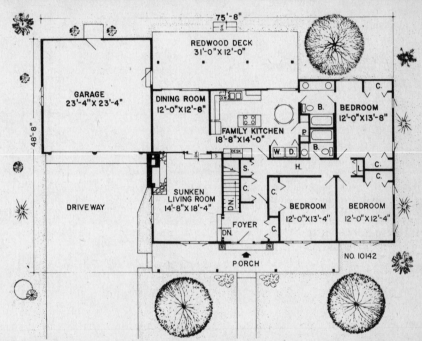

Redwood Bridge Fronts Contemporary

No. 10148

Leading to double entrance doors and a lavish foyer, a redwood bridge expresses the unique, natural flavor of this three-bedroom contemporary. Immediately visible from the foyer is the fireplace, lighting the expansive sunken living room. Redwood deck beyond is accessible through two pairs of sliding glass doors.

First floor—2,050 sq. ft.
Basement—2,050 sq. ft.
Garage—440 sq. ft.

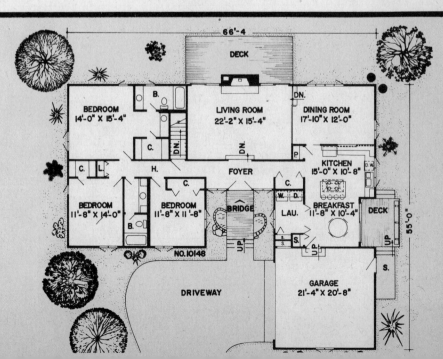

Zoning Effective In Contemporary

No. 10152

Formal living room and foyer serve to zone quiet and active areas in this thoughtfully planned contemporary. Comprising three bedrooms and three full baths, the home displays a floor plan geared to family activities and adaptable to entertaining. Living and family rooms each enjoy wood-burning fireplaces and sliding glass doors to the expansive patio. At front, the kitchen is square and spacious and is flanked by formal dining room and laundry, with storage closet and full bath steps away.

First floor – 1,816 sq. ft.
Basement – 1,816 sq. ft.
Garage – 576 sq. ft.

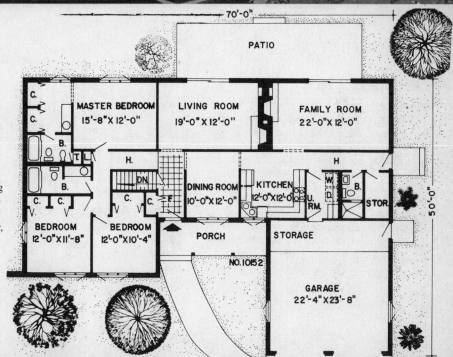

MASTER BEDROOM 15'-8" X 12'-0"

LIVING ROOM 19'-0" X 12'-0"

FAMILY ROOM 22'-0" X 12'-0"

DINING ROOM 10'-0" X 12'-0"

KITCHEN 12'-0" X 12'-0"

BEDROOM 12'-0" X 11'-8"

BEDROOM 12'-0" X 10'-4"

PORCH

STORAGE

PATIO

GARAGE 22'-4" X 23'-8"

70'-0"

50'-0"

NO. 10152

Distinctive Living

No. 8266

An attractive exterior with a most convenient and livable interior. There are three large bedrooms with two full baths. You will enjoy the living room with the interior wall fireplace. The modern built-in kitchen is flanked to the left by the dining room and on the right by a dinette. Note the sliding and folding doors between the kitchen, the dining room and living room. The stairway marked DN leads to the basement which provides more utility space as well as future recreational areas.

First floor — 1,604 sq. ft.
Garage — 455 sq. ft.
Basement — 1,604 sq. ft.

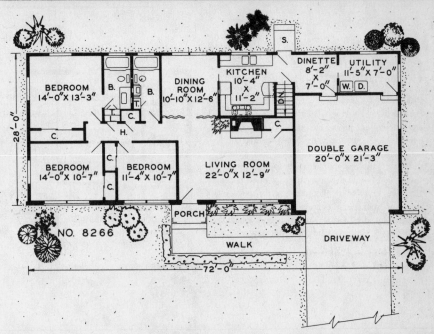

Fireplace Center Of Circular Living Area

No. 10274

A dramatically positioned fireplace forms the focus of the main living area in this single level contemporary. Kitchen, dining, and living rooms form a circle that allows work areas to flow into living areas and outdoors, via sliding glass doors, to the wood deck. Three large bedrooms and two full baths are grouped in a wing away from the living areas. Tucked off the kitchen is a laundry room with closet.

Living area-1,783 sq. ft.
Garage-576 sq. ft.

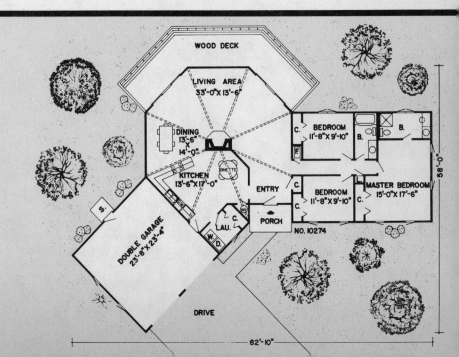

A-Frame Inspires Striking Design

No. 10310

With a facade that suggests a winged A-frame home, this one level plan achieves uniqueness and livability. Notable is the commanding great room with wood-burning fireplace, backed by a firelit family room of identical size. The master bedroom boasts a dressing area, walk-in closets, and private bath, as well as sliding glass doors to its own patio.

First floor-2,090 sq. ft.
Basement-2,090 sq. ft.
Garage-576 sq. ft.

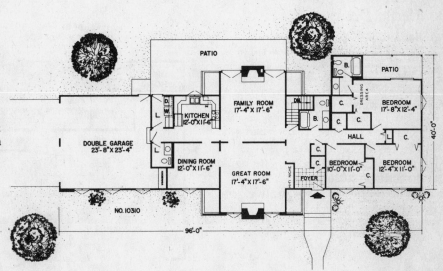

Master Bedroom Merits Deck

No. 10270

Elegantly furnished with private bath and corner tub, the 16-ft. master bedroom in this appealing design opens to a private deck via sliding glass doors. The luxurious design also calls for bay windows in living room and dining room, desk and dining space in the kitchen, and handy workshop off the garage. A full basement, with attached terrace, is provided.

First floor – 2,202 sq. ft.
Basement – 2,016 sq. ft.
Garage/workshop – 864 sq. ft.

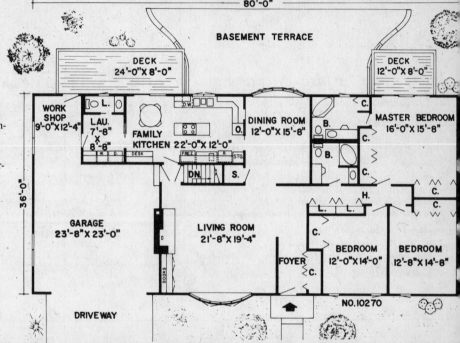

Courtyard Adds Interest To Plan

No. 22010

Well-defined contemporary lines are softened by a semi-enclosed courtyard visible from the dining area of this striking design. The 30-ft. family room is dominated by a fireplace, resulting in a spacious but cozy area for entertaining. The island kitchen merges with dining nook, and bedrooms are large, featuring the master bedroom and its luxurious bath.

House-2,174 sq. ft.
Garage-506 sq. ft.

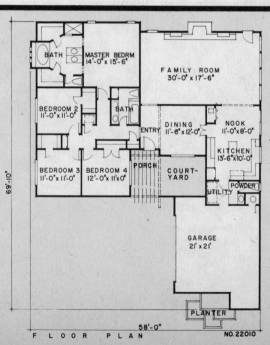

Skylit Family Room Focus Of Plan

No. 22024

Directly accessible from the airy foyer, the 19-ft. family room offers a center for family activity as well as a skylight, fireplace, and sliding glass doors to the adjoining patio. This single level plan groups three bedrooms and two full baths and shows a utility room and dining room. A wet bar edges the dining and family rooms.

House proper-1,974 sq. ft.
Garage-505 sq. ft.

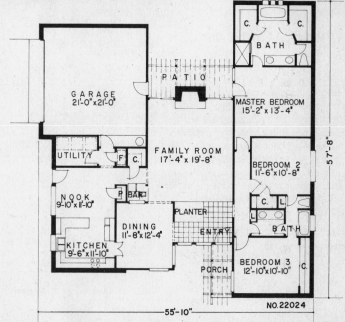

GARAGE
21'-0" x 21'-0"

PATIO

BATH

C.

C.

MASTER BEDROOM
15'-2" x 13'-4"

UTILITY

F. C.

FAMILY ROOM
17'-4" x 19'-8"

BEDROOM 2
11'-6" x 10'-8"

57'-8"

NOOK
9'-10" x 11'-10"

P. BAR

C. L

L

DINING
11'-8" x 12'-4"

PLANTER

ENTRY

BATH

KITCHEN
9'-6" x 11'-10"

PORCH

BEDROOM 3
12'-10" x 10'-10"

C.

55'-10"

NO. 22024

Grillwork, Courtyard, Add Interest

No. 10294

Designed to maximize space and appeal, this four bedroom one level plan begins with a private courtyard introduced by arched grillwork. The sunken living room offers a fireplace and a dead-end arrangement, and dining space is found in the formal dining room as well as the 21-ft. family kitchen. With garage and hall access, the fourth bedroom can serve as guest room, library, or hobby area.

First floor-2,034 sq. ft.
Basement-2,034 sq. ft.
Garage-484 sq. ft.

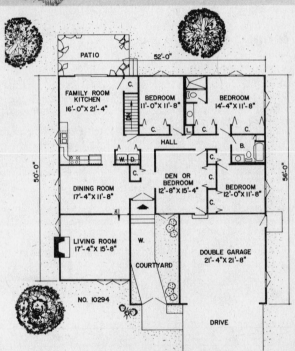

Roofed Terrace Separates Garage, Home

No. 19691

For charm and convenience, a roofed terrace links the garage with this well-arranged ranch style plan. A large living room with fireplace merges with the dining area, and an efficient kitchen includes a pantry. Bordering the kitchen, a nook allots space for dining as well as laundry and sewing equipment. Three bedrooms and two baths, one with sunken tub, are featured.

First floor — 2,136 sq. ft.
Garage — 644 sq. ft.

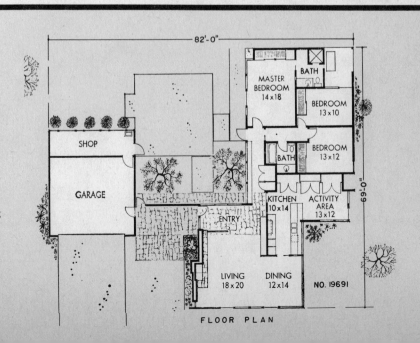

Tasteful Elegance
Aim Of Design

No. 22020

With an exterior that expresses French Provincial charm, this single level design emphasizes elegance and offers a semi-circular dining area overlooking the patio. To pamper parents, the master bedroom annexes a long dressing area and private bath, while another bath serves the second and third bedrooms. A wood-burning fireplace furnishes the family room.

House proper–1,772 sq. ft.
Garage–469 sq. ft.

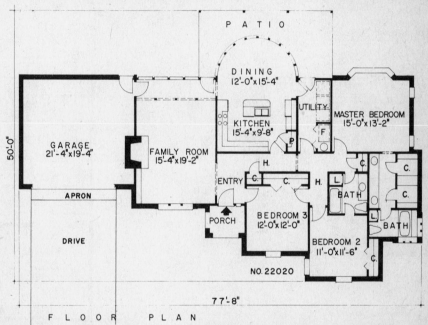

PATIO

DINING
12'-0"x15'-4"

UTILITY

MASTER BEDROOM
15'-0"x13'-2"

KITCHEN
15'-4"x9'-8"

GARAGE
21'-4"x19'-4"

FAMILY ROOM
15'-4"x19'-2"

ENTRY

H.

C.

C.

H.

L

BATH

C.

C.

C.

APRON

PORCH

BEDROOM 3
12'-0"x12'-0"

L

BATH

DRIVE

BEDROOM 2
11'-0"x11'-6"

C.

NO. 22020

50'-0"

77'-8"

FLOOR PLAN

Hip Room Design, Family-centered Space

No. 22008

Inside this trim hip roof plan, space is allotted for a variety of family activities. Spotlighted is the sizable beamed family room with fireplace and access to porch. The bordering gameroom edges a handy half bath, and the dining nook connects to, and visually enlarges, the kitchen. Four bedrooms and two full baths are planned.

House-2,074 sq. ft.
Garage-544 sq. ft.

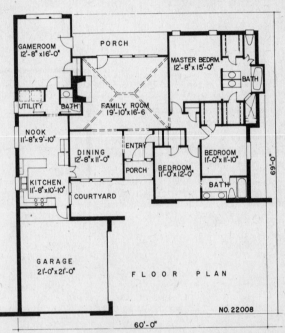

Charming Traditional Emphasizes Living Areas

No. 22014

Besides its 20-ft. family room with fireplace, this one story traditional calls for a dining room, breakfast nook, and sizable gameroom that can function as a formal living room if preferred. Each of the three bedrooms adjoins a full bath, with the master bedroom meriting a luxurious "his and hers" bath with two walk-in closets.

House-2,157 sq. ft.
Garage-485 sq. ft.

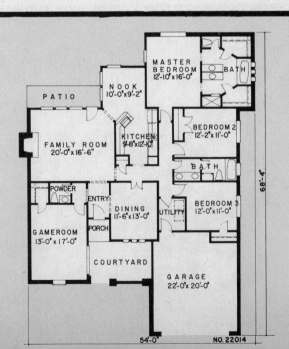

Unique Plan Encircles Atrium

No. 22022

Functional in design, this three bedroom home is enhanced by a central atrium, a restful retreat accessible from hallways and master bedroom. The U-shaped kitchen calls for a built-in pantry, and the neighboring game room includes a wet bar. For family and friends, the spacious living and dining room merits a wood-burning fireplace.

House proper – 1,913 sq. ft.
Garage – 441 sq. ft.
Atrium – 204 sq. ft.

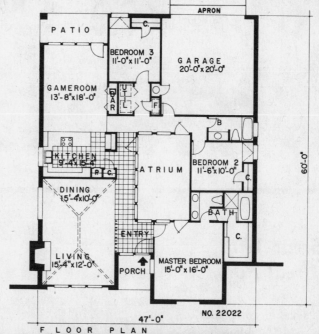

APRON

PATIO

BEDROOM 3
11'-0" x 11'-0"

GARAGE
20'-0" x 20'-0"

GAMEROOM
13'-8" x 18'-0"

BAR UTIL F

B

KITCHEN
9'-4" x 15'-4"

R C

ATRIUM

BEDROOM 2
11'-6" x 10'-0"

C.

DINING
15'-4" x 10'-0"

BATH

ENTRY

C.

LIVING
15'-4" x 12'-0"

PORCH

MASTER BEDROOM
15'-0" x 16'-0"

60'-0"

47'-0"

NO. 22022

FLOOR PLAN

Passive Solar With Unique Great Room

No. 10380

Expanses of glass and rugged exposed beams dominate the front of this design's six-sided living center, creating a contemporary look that would be outstanding in any setting. Angled service and sleeping wings flow to the right and left, creating unusual shaped rooms and leaving nooks and crannies for storage. Spiral stairs just inside the tiled entry rise to a loft overlooking the great room. All rooms have sloping ceilings with R-38 insulation while sidewalls call for R-24. Living and dining possibilities are expanded by use of the rear patio and deck. A full basement lies under the house.

First floor — 2,199 sq. ft.
Loft — 336 sq. ft.
Garage — 611 sq. ft.
Basement — 2,199 sq. ft.

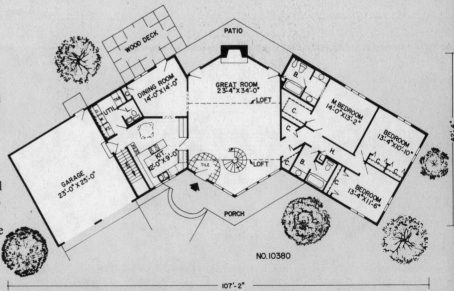

NO. 10380

107'-2"

Open Living Area Highlights Well-zoned Plan

No. 10523

A feeling of spaciousness is created by the centrally located living and dining areas which both have a view of the hearthed fireplace. The galley-style kitchen features a pantry, a bump-out window over the sink, and easy access to the combined laundry/utility room. The breakfast nook, which overlooks the deck, is flooded with light from the uniquely arranged windows. The three bedrooms and two baths are on the other side of the core of activity rooms. The master bedroom has a private bath plus a double vanity, walk-in and a walk-in closet in the dressing area.

First floor — 1737 sq. ft.
Basement — 1737 sq. ft.
Garage — 584 sq. ft.

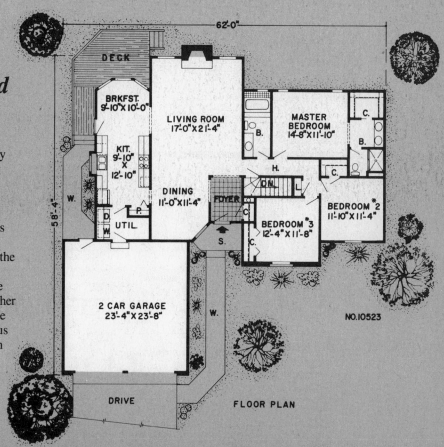

FLOOR PLAN

Angled Design Yields Interesting Shapes

No. 140

Fresh, innovative planning gives birth to a fascinating and unconventionally shaped kitchen, family room, and dining room in this contemporary design. This unique room arrangement also enjoys sliding glass doors to the partially roofed terrace, where a built-in barbecue grill invites outdoor cooking. The formal, fireplace-brightened living room is free of cross traffic. Three bedrooms comprise the sleeping wing, including a sizable master bedroom with private bath and double closets.

First floor — 1,735 sq. ft.
Basement — 1,187 sq. ft.
Garage — 498 sq. ft.

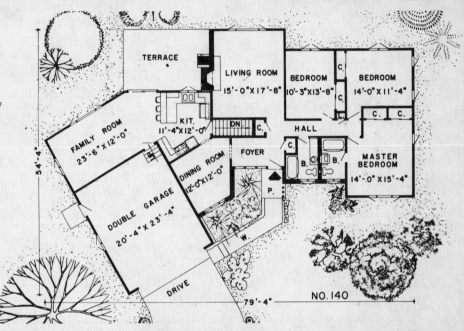

Additions Transform Traditional Plan

No. 152

Intriguing diamond light windows, contrasting siding, and a cupola trim convert this simple ranch style into an appealing design. Its expansive living room enjoys both a fireplace and a terrace, via sliding glass doors. The kitchen is compact and handy to the formal dining room and garage. Three bedrooms comprise the sleeping wing, including a master bedroom with private bath, and a niche is provided for the washer and dryer. Boat storage is included in the extra large garage.

First floor-1,643 sq. ft.
Basement-1,643 sq. ft.
Garage-763 sq. ft.

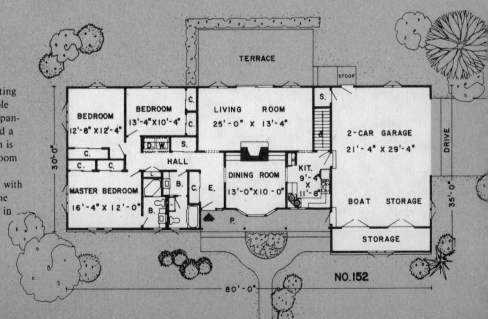

Stone, Brick, Glass
Light Exterior

No. 150

Expanses of glass edge and encircle this L-shaped design and fuse with brick and stone to produce a unique and low maintenance exterior. Country kitchen joins the informal, enjoyable dining area, allots snack bar and laundry space, and serves living room and family room with equal ease. Sliding glass doors open family room to flagstone terrace, while the living room exhibits a cozy corner fireplace. Two large tiled baths, one private to the master bedroom, serve the sleeping area.

First floor — 1,864 sq. ft.
Basement — 1,864 sq. ft.
Garage — 528 sq. ft.

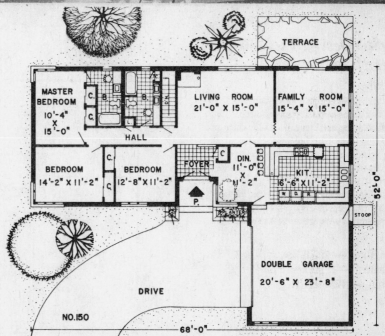

Kitchen Complex Noted for Efficiency

No. 160

Sporting both dining and laundry centers, the kitchen complex in this appealing ranch style serves as a functional unit, handy to living room and family room. Sleeping areas are clearly defined for privacy, especially the separate master bedroom with bath. Tiled entry and hallways channel traffic and allow the living room seclusion and formality. Set behind the garage, the family room provides a large recreation area for active use and opens to the outdoors via sliding glass doors.

First floor — 1,782 sq. ft.
Basement — 1,782 sq. ft.
Garage — 406 sq. ft.

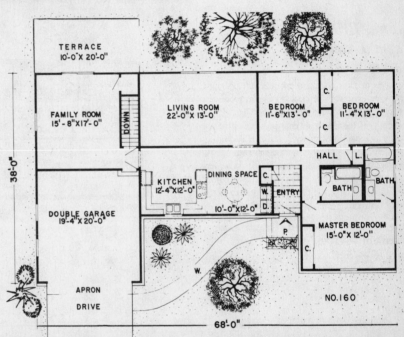

Cut Stone Veneer Attractive

No. 170

The three bedrooms are large with many windows to assure adequate light and proper ventilation. A large walk-in closet and lavatory are shown in the master bedroom. The kitchen is large enough for a breakfast nook as shown and a utility room is provided. If a basement is not desired, the space allotted for the stairs can be used in the kitchen.

First floor — 2,064 sq. ft.
Basement — 2,064 sq. ft.
Garage — 500 sq. ft.

An Exciting Plan That's Full Of Great Features

No. 196

Angled inward to provide relaxation for both master bedroom and family room, the covered patio joins with the screened porch in creating sheltered outdoor offshoots of this contemporary plan. Privacy characterizes the patio, open to the elegant master bedroom with bath and dressing room, while the screened porch adjoins the kitchen and suggests enjoyable outdoor dining. Extending from the kitchen is the airy family room furnished with breakfast bar and fireplace.

First floor-1,805 sq. ft.
Basement-970 sq. ft.
Garage-475 sq. ft.

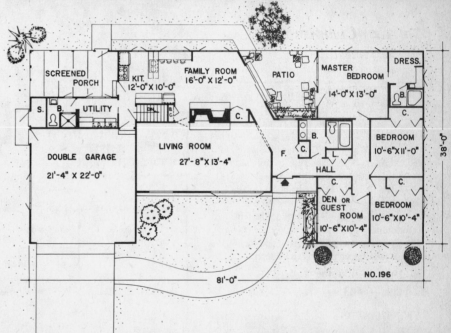

SCREENED PORCH

KIT. 12'-0" X 10'-0"

FAMILY ROOM 16'-0" X 12'-0"

PATIO

MASTER BEDROOM 14'-0" X 13'-0"

DRESS.

S. B. UTILITY

DN.

LIVING ROOM 27'-8" X 13'-4"

DOUBLE GARAGE 21'-4" X 22'-0"

B.

F.

HALL

C.

BEDROOM 10'-6" X 11'-0"

DEN OR GUEST ROOM 10'-6" X 10'-4"

BEDROOM 10'-6" X 10'-4"

38'-0"

81'-0"

NO. 196

An Air of Elegance

No. 242

A sunken living room is featured in this beautiful hipped roof, ranch style house. The entrance foyer is very attractive with its tiled floor and louvered partition next to the breakfast room. The foyer connects to a central hall which efficiently channels traffic to each room. The master bedroom has its own private bath, wood-burning fireplace and walk-in closet. Open planning is the rule in the family room, kitchen area. A long snack bar serves as a divider. The half bath and laundry room are conveniently located near the kitchen area. A barbecue grill is included in the family room, utilizing the living room fireplace chimney. Both living room and family room open onto the covered patio through sliding glass doors.

First floor — 2,227 sq. ft.
Garage — 643 sq. ft.

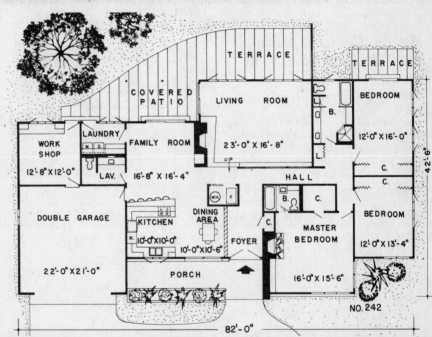

From the Family Room, to the Terrace . . . Relax

No. 288

For the family who likes to entertain, the modern exterior of this home encloses a plan equally as modern. The center hall plan allows movements from the entrance to each of the primary home areas. For gracious entertaining the living room offers an attractive setting and for relaxed informality there is a large family room with a wood-burning fireplace and an attractive snack bar. The half bath is conveniently located near the center of the house.

First floor — 1,775 sq. ft.
Carport — 372 sq. ft.

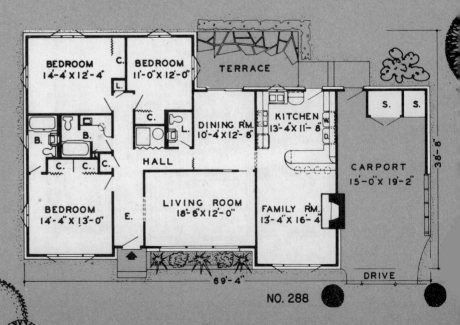

The Ultimate to Living

No. 254

This three bedroom ranch style house was designed for an active family requiring extra large
rooms. The oversized foyer adds an air of luxury
and provides privacy for the living room. A separate dining room is provided so the family room
can be devoted entirely to family living. The master bedroom has its own private bath and two large
closets, both over five feet long. The kitchen contains the washer and dryer and a breakfast bar. A
full basement is included for utilities, storage, etc.

First floor — 1,900 sq. ft.
Basement — 1,900 sq. ft.

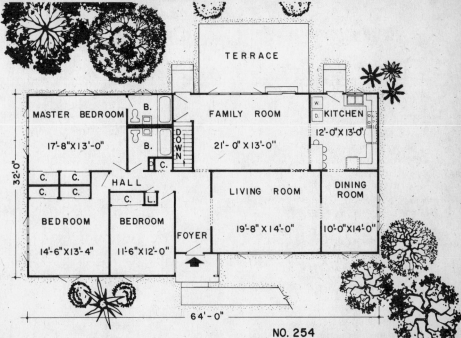

NO. 254

Popular Ranch Design Highlights Family Room

No. 10504

The inviting family room of this home contains its own wet bar, fireplace and opens onto the patio through sliding glass doors. Entertaining will be easy because of the location of the extra large kitchen. The L-shaped kitchen features an island snack bar plus additional space for eat-in convenience. The formal dining and living rooms are joined for a more spacious design and are accented by plenty of windows. The three large bedrooms include large wall closets. One bedroom features mirrored closet doors and separate vanity and shower.

First floor — 1,922 sq. ft.
Garage — 422 sq. ft.

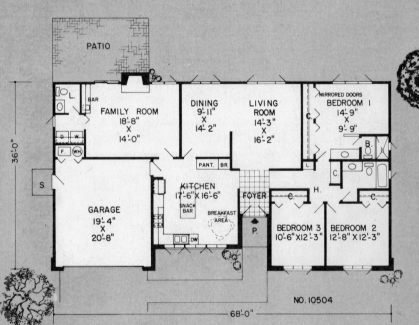

Circular Kitchen Is Center of Family Activities

No. 10514

The unusual design of this kitchen provides the centerpiece for this thoroughly delightful floor plan. The kitchen is further enhanced by the tiled hallways which surround it and delineate the adjacent living areas. The dining room, which opens onto the patio with large glass doors, includes both a built-in hutch and a display case. The large family room has a fireplace with its own wood storage and provides direct access to the sunspace. The master bedroom suite has a private patio, a bay window, five-piece bath, separate vanity and large, walk-in closet.

First floor — 2,098 sq. ft.
Garage — 448 sq. ft.

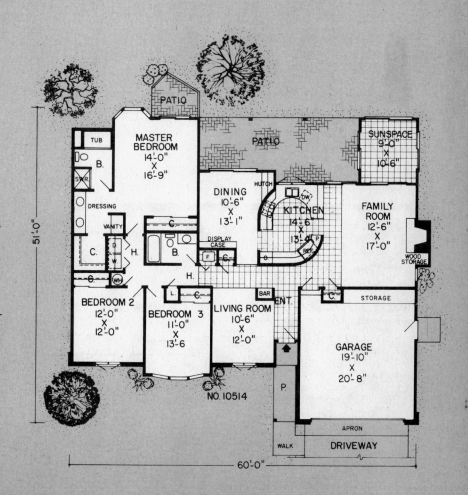

NO. 10514

Bookshelves Line
Living Room

No. 308

Brightened by charming small-paned windows and meriting a television niche flanked by bookshelves, the living room of this comfortable plan offers a haven for quiet relaxation. Formal dining room enjoys access to living room and kitchen, and utility room, useful as a mud room, spans 19 feet to provide room for storage and laundry equipment. Two baths and plenty of closet space characterize the bedroom wing, master bath features shower stall.

First floor — 1,845 sq. ft.
Garage — 436 sq. ft.

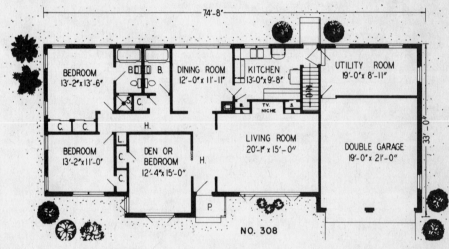

Brick Jackets
Living Room Wall

No. 318

Brick layers the entire wall on the fireplace end of the bow-windowed living room in this attractive home. Tiled foyer circulates traffic to living areas, sleeping areas, and basement. Divided by a long breakfast bar, kitchen and dining rooms are open and spacious, with dining room opening to terrace via sliding glass doors. Four bedrooms are indulged with closets and two tiled baths, while a den borders living areas and is adaptable to playroom or extra bedroom.

First floor — 1,660 sq. ft.
Basement — 1,660 sq. ft.
Garage and workshop — 596 sq. ft.

Stone Chimney Punctuates Exterior

No. 328

Cut stone sheathes the chimney and side of this dignified ranch style and imparts distinction and character to the exterior. Inside, entry is into the large living room, bathed in light from a glowing wood-burning fireplace. Family-dining room beyond opens to terrace via sliding glass doors, and adjoining kitchen complex etches a compact laundry room. Three bedrooms, two full baths, and copious closet space comprise the sleeping area, and master bedroom enjoys a private bath.

First floor — 1,757 sq. ft.
Basement — 1,757 sq. ft.
Garage — 467 sq. ft.

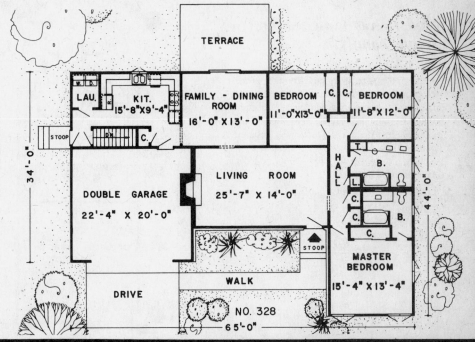

TERRACE

LAU.

KIT.
15'-8" X 9'-4"

FAMILY - DINING ROOM
16'-0" X 13'-0"

BEDROOM
11'-0" X 13'-0"

BEDROOM
11'-8" X 12'-0"

STOOP

DOUBLE GARAGE
22'-4" X 20'-0"

LIVING ROOM
25'-7" X 14'-0"

HALL

B.

MASTER BEDROOM
15'-4" X 13'-4"

STOOP

DRIVE

WALK

NO. 328

34'-0"

44'-0"

65'-0"

Modern Convenience for Young Family

No. 354

Opening off a large foyer, the living room is well separated from the remainder of this home, allowing adults to entertain without being disturbed by children's activities. The kitchen/family room area is divided by a breakfast bar efficiently designed for easy living. Cathedral ceilings are used throughout to provide the extra atmosphere today's young families enjoy.

First floor — 1,738 sq. ft.
Garage — 504 sq. ft.

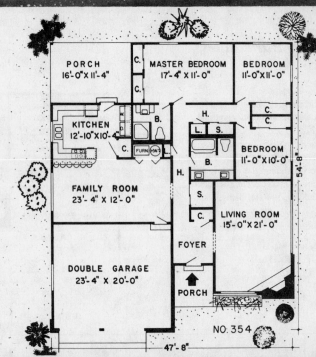

Design Symmetry Enhances Appearance

No. 366

Off at one end of the house, noise made in the family room or garage will not interrupt concentration or sleep in the bedrooms. While children's activities may be confined to the family room, both the living room and dining room are designed for daily use and family lounging. A fireplace in the living room and barbecue grill adjacent to it on the patio add the spark of warmth desired by so many of today's families.

First floor — 1,925 sq. ft.
Basement — 1,925 sq. ft.
Garage — 473 sq. ft.

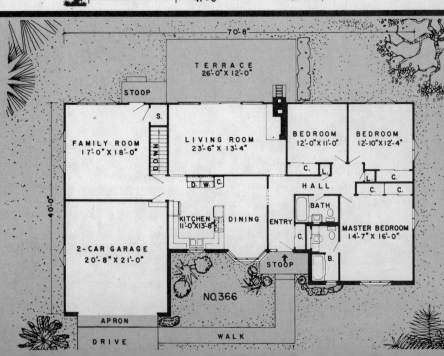

Fireplace Adds Warmth

No. 358

The utility of a well-proportioned living room which opens onto a spacious concrete terrace highlights this attractive house. Over 135 square feet of kitchen space, conveniently situated between laundry and dining rooms, will delight efficient housewives as will the plentiful closet and storage space. Three bedrooms, two full baths and a double garage complete this ranch style home, designated to win the admiration of friends and neighbors.

First floor-1,683 sq. ft.
Basement-1,683 sq. ft.
Garage-453 sq. ft.

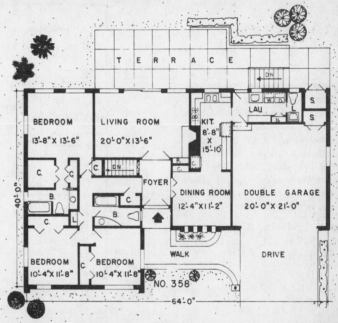

TERRACE

BEDROOM 13'-8" X 13'-6"

LIVING ROOM 20'-0" X 13'-6"

KIT. 8'-8" X 15'-10"

LAU.

FOYER

DINING ROOM 12'-4" X 11'-2"

DOUBLE GARAGE 20'-0" X 21'-0"

BEDROOM 10'-4" X 11'-8"

BEDROOM 10'-4" X 11'-8"

WALK

DRIVE

NO. 358

40'-0"

64'-0"

Sleeping Wing Separate, Restful

No. 386

Maximum quiet and privacy result from the secluded layout of the bedroom wing in this charming ranch style. Four bedrooms are nestled around two full baths, with linen closets and laundry niche adding convenience. Informal family room offers access to basement, terrace, and kitchen. Guests can be accommodated in the 21-foot living room, complete with corner fireplace. For garden equipment, bicycles, and tools, substantial storage space is provided in the double garage.

First floor — 1,649 sq. ft.
Basement — 945 sq. ft.
Garage — 520 sq. ft.

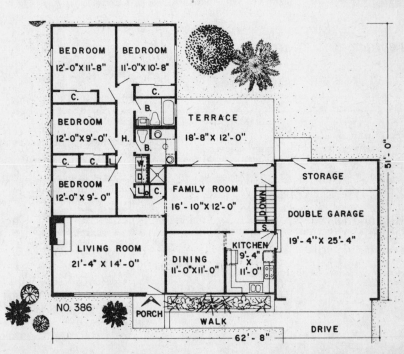

Kitchen Proposes Relaxed Informality

No. 390

Featuring four entrances and an eye-catching angular snack bar, the expansive kitchen-dining area suggests a gathering spot within this three bedroom home. For more formal moments, the design also offers a 24-foot living room with mood set by crackling corner fireplace and sliding glass doors to the terrace. The master bedroom promises comfort and rates double closets and large, private bath with two sinks and towel closet. Sizable utility room bordering the kitchen will solve most storage problems.

First floor — 1,637 sq. ft.
Garage — 420 sq. ft.

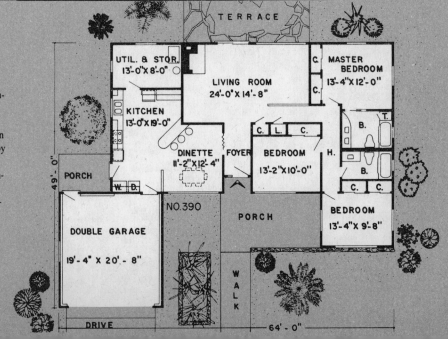

Traditional Boasts Foyer, Closet Space

No. 388

Plentiful closet space favors bedrooms and foyer in this traditionally detailed plan. Arranged for maximum use of space, the floor plan shows a sizable living room off the foyer and a family room-kitchen combination which overlooks, and opens to the terrace. A snack bar serves the area, and bordering 12-foot laundry room is designed to save steps. Three accessible bedrooms are well-closeted and two full baths are placed back to back for construction economy. Additional storage and workshop space abounds in basement and double garage.

First floor — 1,602 sq. ft.
Basement — 1,290 sq. ft.
Garage — 574 sq. ft.

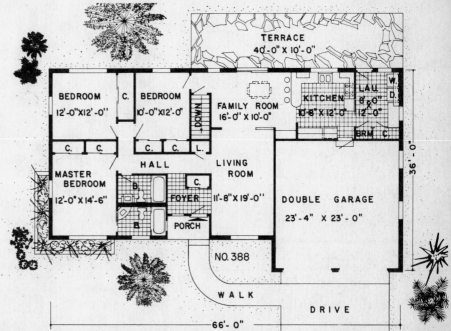

TERRACE 40'-0" X 10'-0"

BEDROOM 12'-0"X12'-0"

BEDROOM 10'-0"X12'-0"

FAMILY ROOM 16'-0" X 10'-0"

KITCHEN 10'-8" X 12'-0"

LAU. 8'-0" 12'-0"

W. D.

BRM C.

36'-0"

MASTER BEDROOM 12'-0" X 14'-6"

HALL

FOYER

LIVING ROOM 11'-8"X19'-0"

DOUBLE GARAGE 23'-4" X 23'-0"

PORCH

NO. 388

WALK

DRIVE

66'-0"

Central Courtyard Features Pool

No. 10507

Created for gracious living, this design is organized around a central courtyard complete with pool. Secluded near one corner of the courtyard is the master bedroom suite which is accented with a skylight, spacious walk-in closet and a bath which also accommodates swimming enthusiasts. The living room, dining room and kitchen occupy another corner. The well located kitchen easily serves the patio for comfortable outdoor entertaining. The family room plus two more bedrooms complete the design.

First floor — 2,194 sq. ft.
Garage — 576 sq. ft.

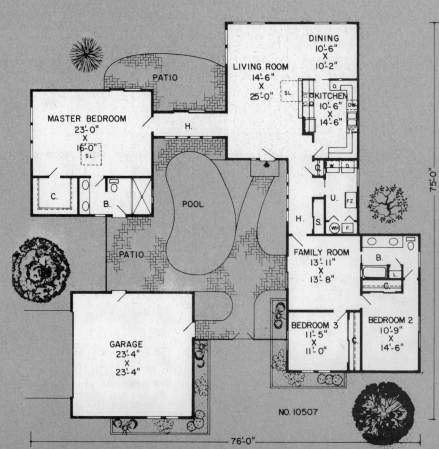

Sunken Living Room Highlights Floor Plan

No. 10508

The semi-circular arrangement of this home accents an open floor plan which uses an elevated hall to separate the living areas. The sunken living room has its own wet bar, built-in bench seat and planters. The family room features a fireplace, built-in bookcases and shares a bar with the adjacent kitchen. The patio area is open to the dining room, kitchen and family room for easy entertaining. The master bedroom also overlooks the patio. Its large bath is divided into compartments and has a large walk-in closet. The other two bedrooms each have their own baths and spacious closets.

First floor — 2,251 sq. ft.
Garage — 533 sq. ft.

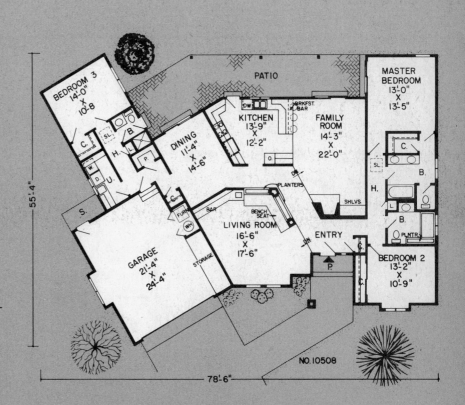

Living, Family Rooms Angled For View

No. 9107

Framed by a redwood balcony, this natural stone and shake shingle design sets living room and family-dining room on an angle and indulges them with windows to capture the view. Sliding glass doors open both rooms to the balcony, and a wood-burning fireplace further equips the family room. Quick meals are possible in the large kitchen, which also allots laundry space. Closeted foyer presents a gracious entrance and all but eliminates cross-traffic through rooms. Four bedrooms and two compartmented baths provide ample sleeping quarters.

First floor – 2,051 sq. ft.
Basement – 1,380 sq. ft.
Garage – 671 sq. ft.

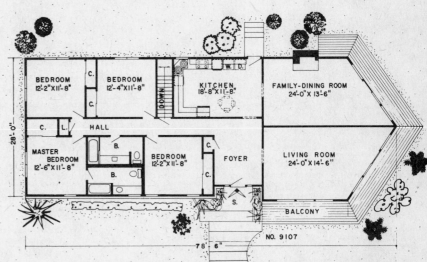

BEDROOM 12'-2"X11'-8"
BEDROOM 12'-4"X11'-8"
KITCHEN 18'-8"X11'-8"
W. D.
DOWN
FAMILY-DINING ROOM 24'-0"X 13'-6"
C.
C.
C. L. HALL
MASTER BEDROOM 12'-6"X11'-8"
B.
BEDROOM 12'-2"X11'-8"
C.
FOYER
LIVING ROOM 24'-0"X14'-6"
B.
C.
S.
28'-0"
BALCONY
78'-6"
NO. 9107

Courtyard Sets Pace For Home

No. 21506

Refreshing in concept, this one story design is reached via a long courtyard that sets a gracious tone. Master bedroom which merits a private bath and dressing area is flanked by two patios. For convenience, a utility room separates the double garage and kitchen. A sizable family room is included.

House — 1,737 sq. ft.
Garage — 452 sq. ft.

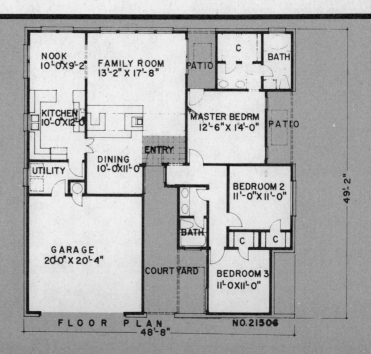

NOOK 10'-0"X9'-2"
FAMILY ROOM 13'-2" X 17'-8"
PATIO
C
BATH
KITCHEN 10'-0"X12'-0"
MASTER BEDRM 12'-6"X 14'-0"
PATIO
UTILITY
DINING 10'-0"X11'-0"
ENTRY
BEDROOM 2 11'-0"X11'-0"
GARAGE 20'-0"X 20'-4"
BATH
C
C
49'-2"
COURTYARD
BEDROOM 3 11'-0"X11'-0"
FLOOR PLAN
48'-8"
NO. 21506

Living Room Set Apart For Formality

No. 9930

Insulated from traffic and activity centers, the expansive living room in this stone-spread ranch style offers a formality and quiet of its own. In the family room, a fireplace engenders a bright and warming atmosphere that can spill out to the terrace via sliding glass doors. A small dining area is situated beyond the kitchen and borders a utility room and half bath. Outstanding in the sleeping wing is the luxury-lined master bedroom with a bath that incorporates "his" and "hers" sinks and a towel closet.

First floor — 1.915 sq.ft.
Basement — 1,915 sq. ft.
Garage — 531 sq. ft.

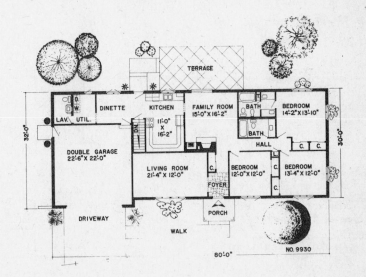

Three Fireplaces
Decorate Home

No. 9514

A fireplace unit provides corner fireplaces for the living and family rooms of this ranch home. The living room incorporates a dining area opening onto the kitchen, complete with breakfast nook. Opening from the garage is a shop or hobby area. Three bedrooms with one and one-half baths complete the sleeping area. In addition to large closets in the bedrooms, a closet in the mudroom and hall and a linen closet in the bathroom give adequate storage room.

First floor — 1,726 sq. ft.
Basement — 1,726 sq. ft.
Garage and shop — 558 sq. ft.

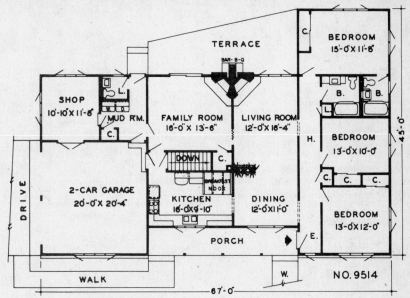

Low Lines Bound
Capacious Interior

No. 9682

Intersecting brick and wood siding clothe the exterior of this low-slung ranch style, which encases a total of five bedrooms and three and one half baths. A cozy family room is favored with sliding glass doors to a flagstone patio that cascades forward on two levels. The half bath is thoughtfully placed, handy to the mud room, kitchen, and family room. Included in the bedroom wing are three full baths and five bedrooms, one of which is fringed with shelves and appropriate for use as a den or children's playroom.

First floor — 2,362 sq. ft.
Basement — 2,362 sq. ft.
Garage — 420 sq. ft.

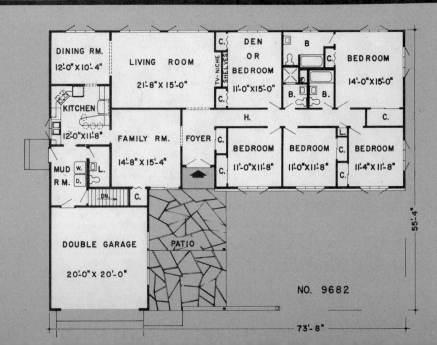

52

This Is Beautiful

No. 9540

This ranch-type house features maximum livability. Four large bedrooms and three full baths are included. The entry is very attractive with the built-in planter serving as a divider between the living room and hall. The cut stone fireplace divides the living room and dining room. The hall bath is compartmented and includes a separate shower and built-in dressing table. The kitchen is large and roomy and contains a built-in range and oven and space for the washer and dryer.

First floor — 2,616 sq. ft.
Basement — 1,897 sq. ft.
Garage — 528 sq. ft.

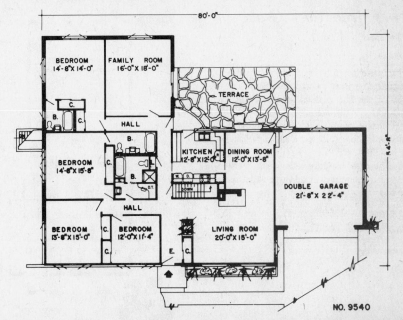

J·R·BRESLER··

Arches, Iron Work Grace One-Story Plan

No. 9386

Brick arches, exposed beams, and intriguing grill-work create a one-story home with a Spanish accent; inside, the floor plan maximizes the single level advantages. The elongated kitchen/dining area can choose informality or partition to form a separate dining room, while the adjoining laundry center is well located to save steps. Served by two full baths, each of the three bedrooms is comfortably large and equipped with adequate closet space. Living and family rooms furnish activity areas.

First floor — 1,695 sq. ft.
Garage — 585 sq. ft.

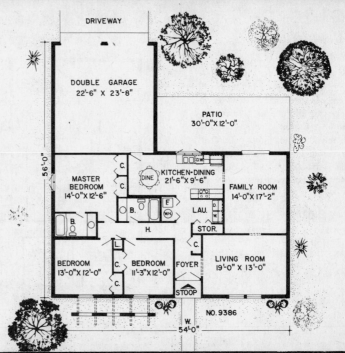

Abundance of Space Enhances Livability

No. 9886

Generously proportioned rooms and open planning result in a considerable amount of space for living in this sleek, brick trimmed design. To the right of the tiled entry, a combination living and dining room measures over 26 feet long, and annexes an even larger family room and kitchen complex with access to the terrace. Even the laundry room is sizable and houses a sink and storage closet. The well planned bedroom wing allots three bedrooms, two full baths, and plentiful closet space.

First floor — 1,881 sq. ft.
Basement — 1,678 sq. ft.
Garage — 590 sq. ft.

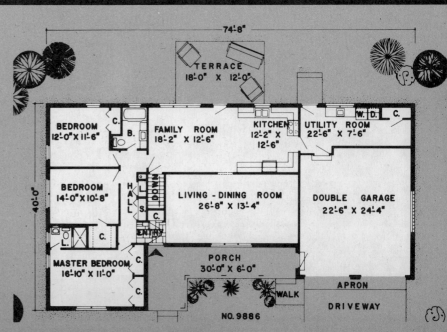

Spanish Accents Create Stately Facade

No. 9394

Gracefully arched windows and doorways and an unusual chimney treatment are among the ornate touches that lend this single level plan its Spanish charm. Accessible from the gracious foyer, the elongated living room provides a substantial area for entertaining guests. Bordering the living room is a formal dining room. A family/dining area serves to focus family activities. Three bedrooms, each with plentiful closet space, and two full baths are shown.

First floor — 1,628 sq. ft.
Garage — 633 sq. ft.

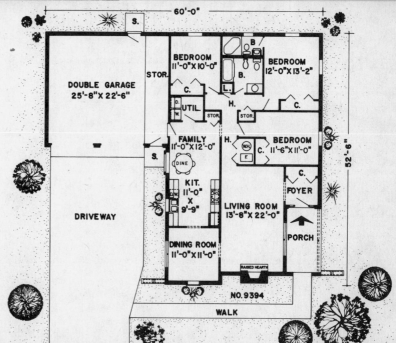

Beamed Ceiling and Corner Fireplace Add Unusual Accents

No. 10506

This home's spacious living room will be enjoyed by guests and family alike. In addition to the beamed ceiling and corner fireplace, it opens onto a large, angled deck and has its own wet bar. The living room also adjoins the dining room and shares an eating bar with the kitchen. This well designed kitchen provides plenty of work space and storage plus room for extra cooks. The three bedrooms complete the floor plan. The master bedroom has a full-wall closet, five-piece bath plus direct access to the deck through sliding glass doors.

First floor — 1,893 sq. ft.
Garage — 494 sq. ft.

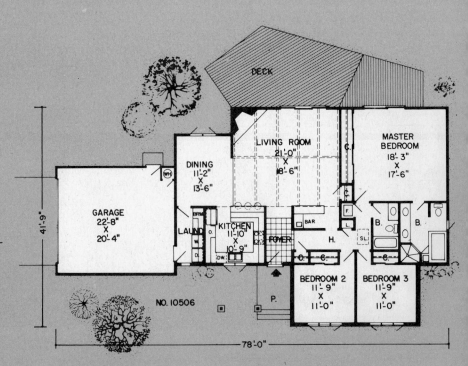

Loft Expands
Modern Design

No. 10516

Above the family room, with its wood-burning stove, this well organized plan tucks in a cozy, sunlit loft. The dining and living rooms have a fireplace and extend into one another to create an atmosphere of spaciousness. The efficient kitchen is conveniently located between the dining room and the family room. The master bedroom suite has its own built-in window seat in the private dressing area which is adjacent to both the bath and the walk-in closet. A home office plus the front courtyard complete this comfortable design.

First floor — 1,930 sq. ft.
Loft — 218 sq. ft.
Garage — 506 sq. ft.

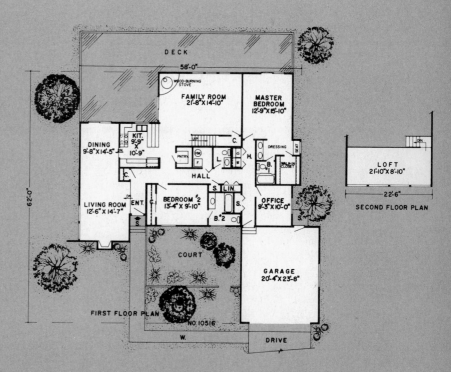

Courtyard Plan Given Contemporary Slant

No. 10130

Sprawling and lavish, this unusual contemporary plan displays a walled courtyard and surrounds a patio and atrium with pool. Sliding glass doors open the atrium to all sections of the home and create a pleasant fusion of indoors and outdoors. Views of the pool are especially enjoyed by beamed, firelit living room at right and large, eat-in kitchen above. Three bedrooms border the long, compartmented bath, and a closed-off laundry center adjoins the kitchen.

First floor — 1,734 sq. ft.
Patio & atrium — 292 sq. ft.
Garage — 592 sq. ft.

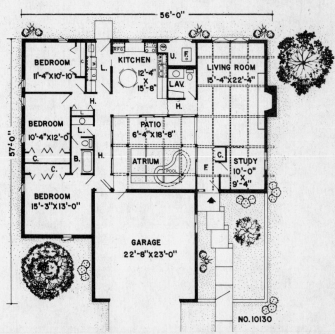

Open Plan Asset in Distinctive Home

No. 10144

Expansive and spacious, this stone-trimmed four bedroom design uses open planning to its fullest advantage. Rooms, even bathrooms, are large, and dining and family rooms increase space with the use of sliding glass doors opening to deck and patio. The large foyer offers access to all areas of the home.

First floor — 2,086 sq. ft.
Basement — 2,086 sq. ft.
Garage — 831 sq. ft.

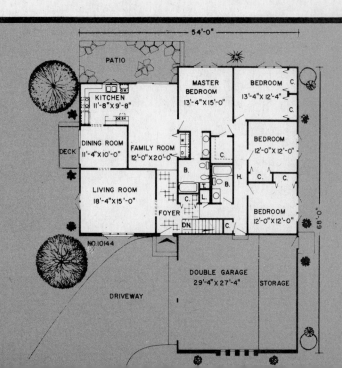

Double Doors Create Inviting Facade

No. 396

Welcoming guests into the flagstone foyer, the double doors of this attractive home create an inviting atmosphere that is carried through on the interior. An efficient floor plan places utility room and eat-in kitchen at right, with living and dining rooms adjoining. Open to the foyer, the 24-foot living room joins the formal dining room to provide party space, and the dining room annexes the terrace via sliding glass doors. The bedroom wing benefits from two full baths and ample closet space, including a large utility closet with built-in shelves.

First floor — 1,686 sq. ft.
Garage — 360 sq. ft.

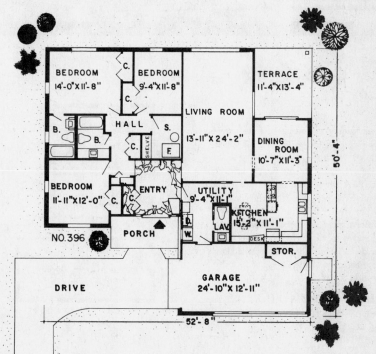

BEDROOM 14'-0"X11'-8"

BEDROOM 9'-4"X11'-8"

TERRACE 11'-4"X13'-4"

HALL

LIVING ROOM 13'-11"X24'-2"

DINING ROOM 10'-7"X11'-3"

BEDROOM 11'-11"X12'-0"

ENTRY

UTILITY 9'-4"X11'-1"

KITCHEN 15'-2"X11'-1"

LAV.

PORCH

NO. 396

STOR.

DRIVE

GARAGE 24'-10"X12'-11"

50'-4"

52'-8"

Kitchen Complex Unique, Functional

No. 1002

Nothing succeeds like convenience in the cooking-dining-relaxing complex of this brick-sheathed three bedroom ranch style. Appendaging a den or family room, breakfast room, laundry niche and snack bar, the kitchen complex becomes a unique family center with access to front entry and carport. For guests, the adjoining dining and living rooms preserve formality and avoid cross-traffic. Three bedrooms include a 16-foot master bedroom, handsomely furnished with double closets and private bath. Two hall closets and a utility room serve the sleeping area.

First floor — 1,765 sq. ft.
Carport — 360 sq. ft.
Storage — 144 sq. ft.

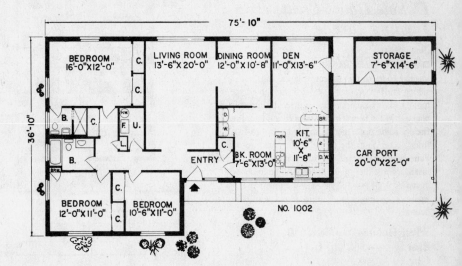

A Proven Plan

No. 9024

A beautiful hipped roof, brick and stone veneer ranch home. Two large bedrooms with baths, one with tub and one with shower. Each of these rooms has two large closets. There is a third bedroom and still a fourth which may be used as a den or a bedroom. The hallway leads from the front entrance back to and through the kitchen to the rear entrance. Note the large living room and the large family room, each with a fireplace. The family room is provided with folding doors to divide the room if desired and it is also provided with a half bath.

First floor — 2,509 sq. ft.
Basement — 2,509 sq. ft.
Garage — 432 sq. ft.

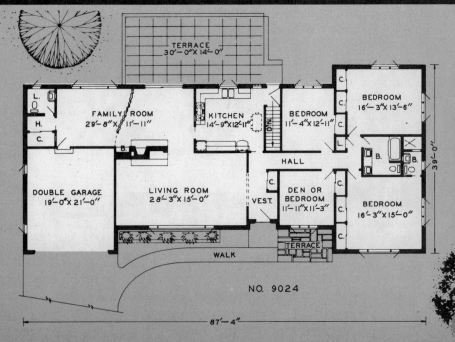

Family Room Accessible from Two Sides

No. 8302

Directly accessible to the kitchen and rear entrance, the family room in this brick and vertical siding-trimmed ranch style also opens to the bedroom hallway, making it doubly useful as child's playroom and informal entertaining center. Restful fires glow in the living room, partially divided from the dining room by a decorative planter. Functional and open, the kitchen chooses a breakfast bar to the dining room, and the entire area is open to the side porch through sliding glass doors. Walk-in closet and full bath benefit the master bedroom.

First floor — 1,568 sq. ft.
Basement — 1,568 sq. ft.
Garage — 587 sq. ft.

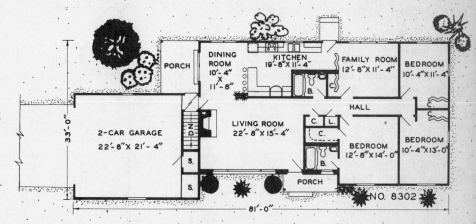

Laundry Nook Adds Convenience

No. 9078

Opening from the kitchen and double garage is a large work room. Designed with a cut stone front, the home is ideal for entertaining. A foyer provides direct access to the family room, adjacent to the kitchen and rear terrace. Providing added convenience are a full basement and formal dining room. Three bedrooms, with two full baths, open onto a hall, hidden from main traffic areas of the house.

First floor — 1,855 sq. ft.
Basement — 1,762 sq. ft.
Garage and storage — 565 sq. ft.

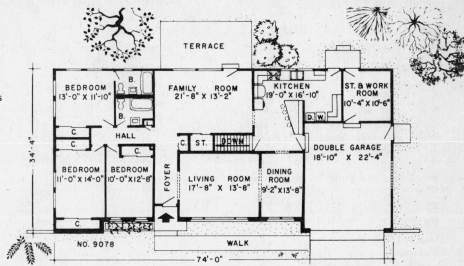

Chimney Commands Contemporary Exterior

No. 9662

Indicative of glowing log fires within, the chimney dominates and enriches the exterior of this three bedroom contemporary home. Expanses of windows are shaded by overhangs and admit light without glaring sun. Inside, living room and family room are favored with fireplaces to spark formal or informal gatherings. Open kitchen and dining room borders a mud room that doubles as laundry, and half bath and storage room complete the area. Master bedroom is furnished with two closets and full bath, and highly efficient hall bath features double sinks, tub and shower stall.

First floor — 1,903 sq. ft.
Basement — 1,792 sq. ft.
Garage and storage — 536 sq. ft.

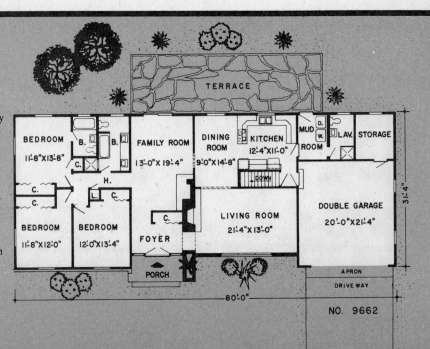

Ranch Has Exceptional Plan

No. 9092

All rooms except the kitchen are accessible from the center hall. Plenty of light and ventilation are provided in all rooms. The living room and family room both have massive areas of glass. There are both inside and outside stairways to the basement. The kitchen is nicely arranged with space for eating and also for the washer and dryer. The rectangular shape of the house assures economy of construction.

First floor — 1,670 sq. ft.
Basement — 1,670 sq. ft.
Garage — 570 sq. ft.

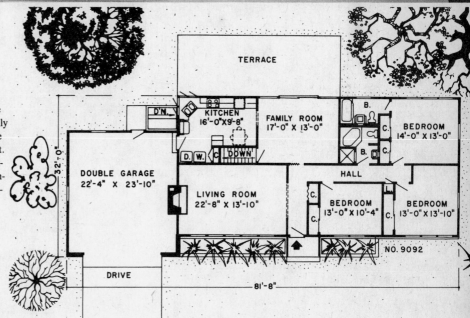

TERRACE

KITCHEN
16'-0" X 9'-8"

FAMILY ROOM
17'-0" X 13'-0"

B.

BEDROOM
14'-0" X 13'-0"

D'N.

D.W.

DOWN

DOUBLE GARAGE
22'-4" X 23'-10"

LIVING ROOM
22'-8" X 13'-10"

HALL

BEDROOM
13'-0" X 10'-4"

BEDROOM
13'-0" X 13'-10"

NO. 9092

32'-0"

DRIVE

81'-8"

J. R. BRESLER

Outstanding Plan Shows Sunken Family Room

No. 22016

Contemporary in its approach to family living, this single level design equips its sunken family room with wood-burning fireplace and sliding glass doors to the patio. Country kitchen and garage are separated by a laundry/mud room, and a formal dining room is offered. Notable is the master bedroom, with its large areas of wall space and private bath with walk-in closet.

House-1,880 sq. ft.
Garage-524 sq. ft.

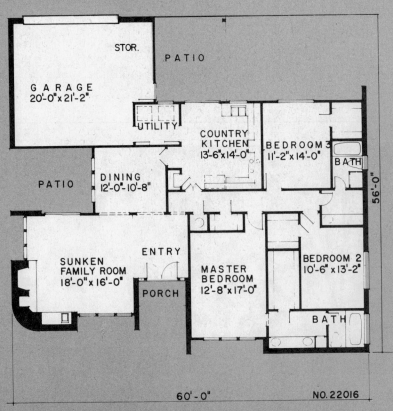

STOR.

PATIO

GARAGE
20'-0" x 21'-2"

UTILITY

COUNTRY KITCHEN
13'-6" x 14'-0"

BEDROOM 3
11'-2" x 14'-0"

BATH

PATIO

DINING
12'-0"-10'-8"

SUNKEN FAMILY ROOM
18'-0" x 16'-0"

ENTRY

MASTER BEDROOM
12'-8" x 17'-0"

BEDROOM 2
10'-6" x 13'-2"

PORCH

BATH

56'-0"

60'-0"

NO. 22016

Effective Zoning
Marks Design

No. 22018

Bedrooms, family living areas, and formal dining room are carefully defined and separated in this well-zoned plan. Three bedrooms cluster around two full baths at right, while the left wing spotlights a family room, hallway, and dining room that encircle and overlook the patio. Closets are plentiful throughout.

House proper — 1,879 sq. ft.
Garage — 471 sq. ft.

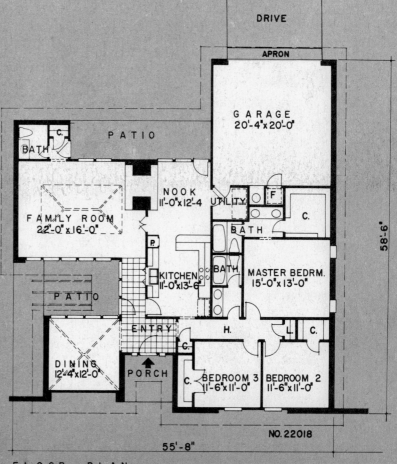

DRIVE

APRON

GARAGE
20'-4" x 20'-0"

PATIO

BATH

C.

NOOK
11'-0" x 12'-4

UTILITY

F

C.

FAMILY ROOM
22'-0" x 16'-0"

BATH

BATH

MASTER BEDRM.
15'-0" x 13'-0"

P

KITCHEN
11'-0" x 13'-6"

58'-6"

PATIO

ENTRY

H.

C.

DINING
12'-4" x 12'-0"

PORCH

C.

C.

BEDROOM 3
11'-6" x 11'-0"

BEDROOM 2
11'-6" x 11'-0"

NO. 22018

55'-8"

FLOOR PLAN

A Practical Plan Throughout

No. 9814

A low maintenance exterior is provided on this home by specifying brick veneer and a cedar shake shingle roof. The hip roof eliminates all gable ends for additional maintenance savings. A very practical floor plan shows three bedrooms, extra large closets and two and one-half baths. The family room, while also serving as the dining room, is large enough for TV viewing and family activities. A full basement provides plenty of space for a large recreation area as well as storage and utility space.

First floor — 1,798 sq. ft.
Basement — 1,798 sq. ft.
Garage — 476 sq. ft.

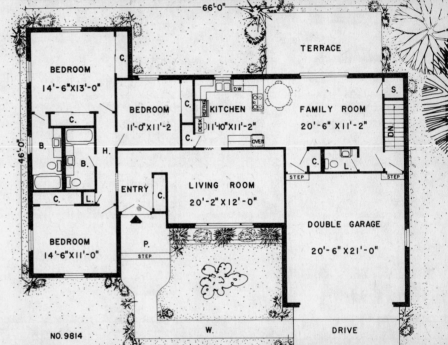

Home Recalls Southern Plantation

No. 9850

Magnificent white columns, shutters, and small paned windows combine to create images of the pre-Civil War South in this generously-proportioned design. Inside, the opulent master bedroom suite, with plentiful closet space, a full bath and study, suggests modern luxury. Fireplaces enhance the formal living room and sizable family room, which skirts the lovely screened porch. The formal dining room boasts built-in china closets.

First floor – 2,466 sq. ft.
Basement – 1,447 sq. ft.
Garage – 664 sq. ft.

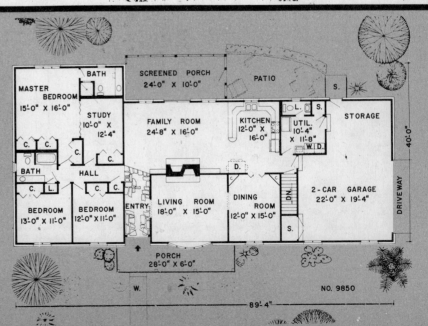

Country Kitchen Boasts Barbecue Grill

No. 9830

Quaint and colorful, the country kitchen of this hipped-roof home is favored with a built-in barbecue and a breakfast bar that separates it from the family room. Carefully detailed, the plan assigns the family room sliding glass doors to take advantage of the triangular terrace and the well-windowed living room a pleasurable wood-burning fireplace. Bedrooms are placed to the rear of the design and include a nicely-proportioned master bedroom with bath, two more substantial bedrooms, and a slightly smaller den.

First floor-1,782 sq. ft.
Basement-1,782 sq. ft.
Garage-576 sq. ft.

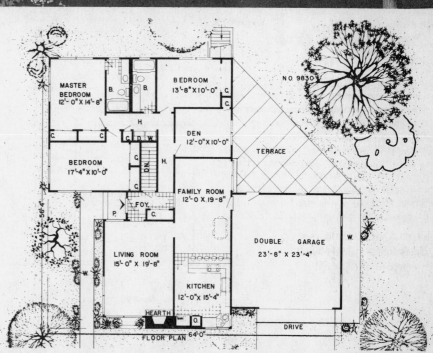

MASTER BEDROOM 12'-0" X 14'-8"

BEDROOM 13'-8" X 10'-0"

NO 9830

TERRACE

DEN 12'-0" X 10'-0"

BEDROOM 17'-4" X 10'-0"

FAMILY ROOM 12'-0 X 19'-8"

FOY.

DOUBLE GARAGE 23'-8" X 23'-4"

LIVING ROOM 15'-0" X 19'-8"

KITCHEN 12'-0" X 15'-4"

HEARTH

DRIVE

FLOOR PLAN 64'-0"

Dressing Room Favors Master Bedroom

No. 9911

Clean traditional lines, brick, and diamond light windows encase a design that specializes in modern comforts and includes a master bedroom with double closets, bath, and dressing room. In all, four generous bedrooms and two full baths comprise the sleeping quarters. Kitchen and family room work together, divided by breakfast bar, and adjoining dining room opens to terrace. Wood-burning fireplaces glow in both family room and living room, arranged for quiet and formality.

First floor — 2,044 sq. ft.
Basement — 2,044 sq. ft.
Garage — 572 sq. ft.

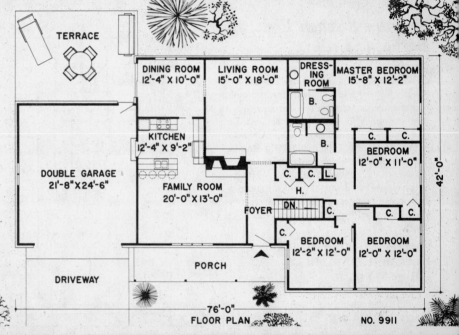

TERRACE

DINING ROOM 12'-4" X 10'-0"

LIVING ROOM 15'-0" X 18'-0"

DRESS-ING ROOM

MASTER BEDROOM 15'-8" X 12'-2"

B.

KITCHEN 12'-4" X 9'-2"

C. C.

BEDROOM 12'-0" X 11'-0"

DOUBLE GARAGE 21'-8" X 24'-6"

B.

C. C. L.

FAMILY ROOM 20'-0" X 13'-0"

H.

FOYER

DN.

C.

C. C.

C.

BEDROOM 12'-2" X 12'-0"

BEDROOM 12'-0" X 12'-0"

DRIVEWAY

PORCH

42'-0"

76'-0"

FLOOR PLAN

NO. 9911

Nature Emphasized in Rambling Plan

No. 9924

Rough-hewn redwood siding and brick exterior fuses with water fountain-accented atrium to concoct a design that blends with nature and stresses interior livability. Closet-lined foyer steers traffic to formal living room with fireplace and terrace as well as to informal living areas. Kitchen and breakfast nook, separated by snack bar, open to another terrace, while the elongated family room merits sliding glass doors to the atrium. Four bedrooms, including master bedroom with dressing area and compartmented bath, comprise the sleeping wing.

First floor — 2,533 sq. ft.
Basement — 2,533 sq. ft.
Garage — 559 sq. ft.

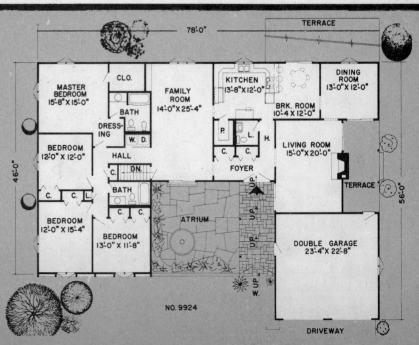

TERRACE

78'-0"

MASTER BEDROOM 15'-8" X 15'-0"

CLO.

FAMILY ROOM 14'-0" X 25'-4"

KITCHEN 13'-8" X 12'-0"

DINING ROOM 13'-0" X 12'-0"

BATH

BRK. ROOM 10'-4 X 12'-0"

BEDROOM 12'-0" X 12'-0"

DRESS-ING

W. D.

P.

L.

LIVING ROOM 15'-0" X 20'-0"

HALL

C.

C. C.

H.

46'-0"

C. C. L.

DN.

FOYER

TERRACE

56'-0"

BATH

UP

BEDROOM 12'-0" X 15'-4"

C. C.

UP

DOUBLE GARAGE 23'-4" X 22'-8"

BEDROOM 13'-0" X 11'-8"

ATRIUM

UP

UP

W.

UP

NO. 9924

DRIVEWAY

Fountain is a Highlight

No. 9922

Imagine a colorful water fountain with automatic changing colored lights located on your front terrace. It will be enjoyed by passers-by as well as people seated in the living room. This is only one of many desirable features found in this beautiful four bedroom home. The large well planned kitchen is located between the formal dining room and the family room. The family room has a wood burning fireplace and a laundry niche for the washer and dryer. The master bedroom has its own private bath and three large closets.

First floor — 2,261 sq. ft.
Basement — 2,261 sq. ft.
Garage — 535 sq. ft.

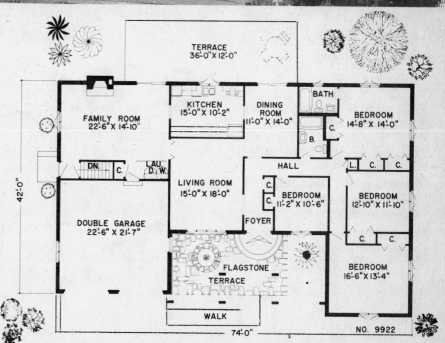

TERRACE
36'-0" X 12'-0"

BATH

KITCHEN
15'-0" X 10'-2"

DINING ROOM
11'-0" X 14'-0"

BEDROOM
14'-8" X 14'-0"

FAMILY ROOM
22'-6" X 14'-10"

C.

B.

DN. C.

LAU.
D. W.

HALL

L. C. C.

LIVING ROOM
15'-0" X 18'-0"

C.

BEDROOM
11'-2" X 10'-6"

BEDROOM
12'-10" X 11'-10"

C.

DOUBLE GARAGE
22'-6" X 21'-7"

FOYER

C. C.

C.

42'-0"

FLAGSTONE
TERRACE

BEDROOM
16'-6" X 13'-4"

C.

WALK

74'-0"

NO. 9922

Stone, Brick Texture Rustic Facade

No. 9382

Battened plywood siding, fieldstone, and textured brick layer the facade of this roomy ranch style to create an exterior with rugged appeal. Entry is across the covered porch into a gracious foyer with living room at left and formal dining room at right to facilitate entertaining.

First floor — 2,440 sq. ft.
Basement — 2,440 sq. ft.
Garage — 578 sq. ft.

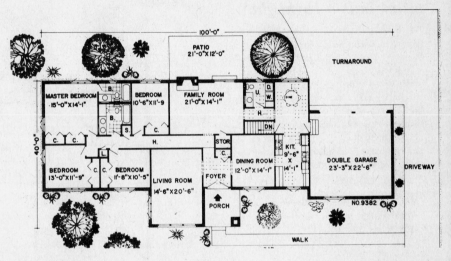

Stone Exterior Requires Little Care

No. 9874

Natural materials are the key to this four bedroom home. The stone veneer requires little mainte-nance, the lovely stone terrace grants a remarkable view, and the wood-burning fireplace cuts the chill on winter evenings. Two full baths and walk-in closets, plus a lounge area in the master bedroom, add to the luxurious air of the sleeping area. The kitchen opens onto a mudroom entering the ga-rage. The center hall plan preserves privacy and directs traffic to living and bedroom areas.

First floor — 2,244 sq. ft.
Basement — 2,244 sq. ft.
Garage — 591 sq. ft.

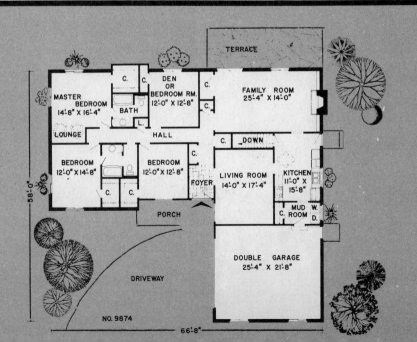

Living Room Sparkles With Light, Warmth

No. 9946

Cathedral ceilings terminating in gable end windows blend with rough cedar beams and a wood-burning fireplace to design a unique living room, alive with light and atmosphere. Natural stone, shake shingles and rough cedar layer the exterior of this singular contemporary. Inside, the living room is nestled near bedrooms for quiet, while activity centers fill the area behind the foyer. Open family room and kitchen enjoy breakfast bar and wooden deck, while a compact laundry and half bath separates kitchen and dining room.

First floor — 2,096 sq. ft.
Basement — 2,096 sq. ft.
Garage — 624 sq. ft.

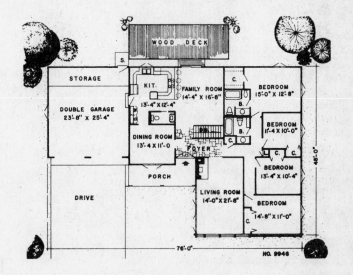

Contemporary Ranch Design

No. 26740

Sloping cathedral ceilings are found throughout the entirety of this home. A kitchen holds the central spot in the floor plan. It is partially open to a great hall with firebox and deck access on one side, daylight room lit by ceiling glass and full length windows on another, and entryway hallway on a third. The daylight room leads out onto a unique double deck. Bedrooms lie to the outside of the plan. Two smaller bedrooms at the rear share a full bath. The more secluded master bedroom at the front has its own full bath and access to a private deck.

Main floor — 1,512 sq. ft.
Garage — 478 sq. ft.

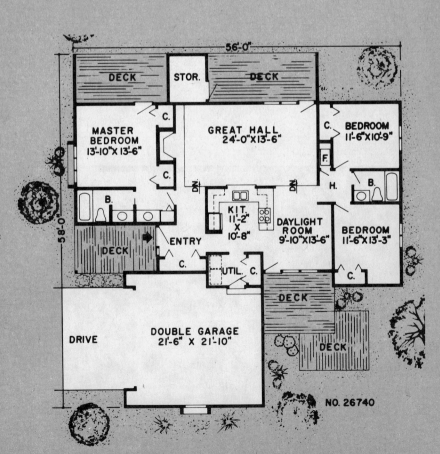

Unusual Design Creates Comfortable Living

No. 26760

The central focus of this highly pleasing 3 bedroom rancher is the family room, its largest most architecturally interesting space. The first room seen upon entering, this room features a prow shape, a beamed ceiling and a fireplace. Sliding glass doors give access to the multi-leveled deck. The well designed kitchen has a center work island and large breakfast area overlooking the deck. The dining room and living room are conveniently placed for ease of entertaining. The master bedroom has a private bath and dressing room. Also included are plenty of closets and a private deck. Two smaller bedrooms share a spacious bath.

Living area-2,000 sq. ft. (excluding decks)

64'

45'

DECK

DECK

DECK

ST.

P.R.

LND

KIT.

BRKFST

FAMILY
15' X 23'

B.

MASTER
BEDRM.
14' X 16'

DINING
13'-3" X 12'

LIVING
15'-9" X 13'

ENT.

SKYL.

STUDY-
BEDRM.
11' X 13'-6"

B.

BEDRM.
11'-6" X 11'-6"

NO. 26760

Private Deck for Sunning or Relaxing

No. 9980

Mediterranean styling is quite prevalent in this beautiful family home. The exterior features a walled veranda or courtyard entrance, arched windows, exposed rafter ends and projecting beams made of rough cedar, shake shingled roof and antique brick. At the rear is a wood deck which wraps around the corner, thereby providing a shady area most of the time. Sliding glass doors in the family room and den open onto the deck. The den is intended to be a sitting room for the master bedroom as well as a den.

First floor — 2,264 sq. ft.
Basement — 2,264 sq. ft.
Garage — 615 sq. ft.

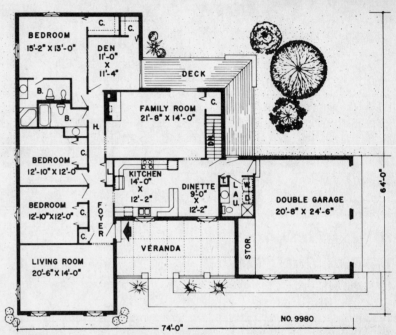

Simplicity Sparks Spanish Design

No. 10008

Fusing Spanish arches with a stark simplicity evokes a dramatic exterior that previews the impressive floor plan of this brick and stucco design. Entry is into the gracious foyer with an arresting view of the sunken living room's wood-burning fireplace. Exposed wood beams accent the ceiling of the room, adjacent to the firelit family room with access to the terrace. An extended kitchen offers a pantry and dining space and borders a convenient half bath. Four bedrooms are outlined, including a lavish master bedroom with closet-lined dressing area and compartmented bath.

First floor — 2,672 sq. ft.
Basement — 2,672 sq. ft.
Garage — 576 sq. ft.

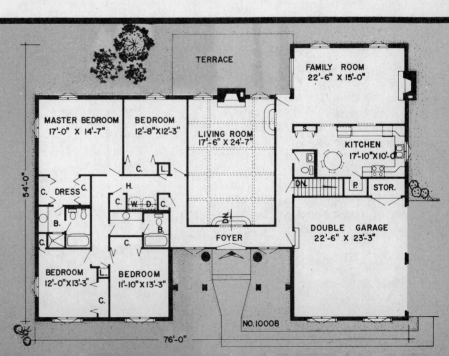

Courtyard Provides Impressive Entry

No. 10000

Outstanding Mediterranean style homes, like this one, are in demand. The courtyard has massive beams overhead which make a very impressive entrance. The stone arch over the living room window, arched garage doors, exposed gable and beams and textured battened siding add further to the beauty of this home. The floor plan is equally outstanding. The formal living room is sunken, has cathedral ceilings and several large exposed beams. The paneled family room has an extra large wood-burning fireplace and sliding glass doors which open onto a large terrace. There are three bedrooms and 2½ baths. The master bedroom is quite elegant.

First floor — 2,103 sq. ft.
Basement — 1,807 sq. ft.
Garage — 569 sq. ft.

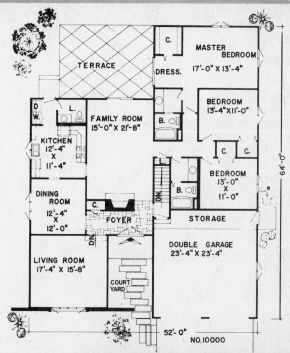

TERRACE

C.

MASTER BEDROOM
17'-0" X 13'-4"

DRESS.

BEDROOM
13'-4" X 11'-0"

B.

FAMILY ROOM
15'-0" X 21'-8"

L.

D W

KITCHEN
12'-4" X 11'-4"

C. C.

BEDROOM
13'-0" X 11'-0"

B.

DINING ROOM
12'-4" X 12'-0"

C.

FOYER

DN

STORAGE

64'-0"

LIVING ROOM
17'-4" X 15'-8"

DN

COURT YARD

DOUBLE GARAGE
23'-4" X 23'-4"

52'-0"

NO. 10000

Have a Hobby and the Room

No. 10014

This three bedroom ranch design will be economical to build and easy to maintain. The hipped roof eliminates all gable ends, eliminating that painting problem. The brick veneer adds esthetic value and requires very little care. The floor plan features an excellent traffic pattern. Notice how all bathroom and laundry plumbing is grouped together for maximum installation economy. There is a hobby room behind the garage.

First floor — 1,383 sq. ft.
Hobby room — 238 sq. ft.
Garage — 485 sq. ft.

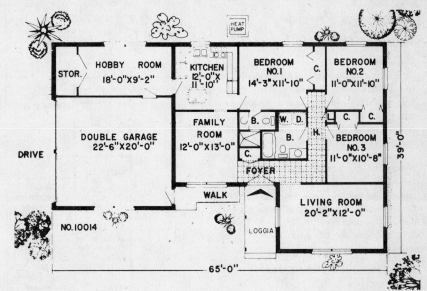

Roof Combination Yields Unique Facade

No. 10030

Combining gable and mansard roof styles accented by a stone chimney produces a memorable facade in this sprawling design. Living room is singled out for the gable roof and also merits cathedral ceilings, gable end windows, exposed beams and wood-burning fireplace. Dining room is separate and augments kitchen eating space, and cozy family room opens to kitchen and terrace. Luxury is expressed in the master bedroom, which features compartmented bath and huge walk-in closet.

First floor — 2,090 sq. ft.
Basement — 2,090 sq. ft.
Garage — 528 sq. ft.

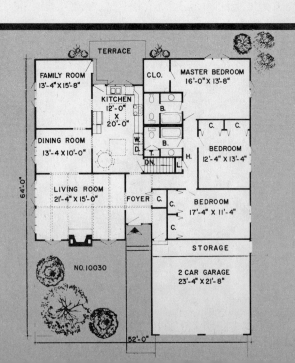

Atrium Illuminates
Entire Home

No. 10028

Emerging as the central point of this contemporary home, the atrium exhibits an ornamental water fountain and the atrium floods much of the home with natural light. Walled mostly in glass, it transmits daylight and starlight to the kitchen, dining room, and the family room which is edged by a terrace. A formal living room is isolated toward the front of the design, as is the master bedroom suite featuring bath, built-in vanity and walk-in closet.

First floor — 2,148 sq. ft.
Basement — 768 sq. ft.
Atrium — 380 sq. ft.
Garage — 576 sq. ft.

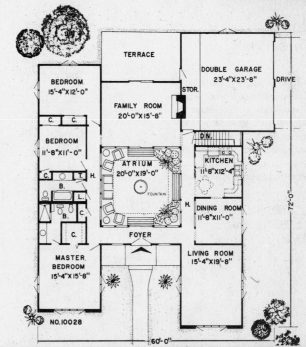

TERRACE

BEDROOM 15'-4"x12'-0"

DOUBLE GARAGE 23'-4"x23'-8"

DRIVE

STOR.

FAMILY ROOM 20'-0"x15'-8"

BEDROOM 11'-8"x11'-0"

DN.

C.   C.

ATRIUM 20'-0"x19'-0"

KITCHEN 11'-8"x12'-4"

FOUNTAIN

72'-0"

H.   T.   H.

B.

L.

DINING ROOM 11'-8"x11'-0"

B.   C.

H.

C.

FOYER

MASTER BEDROOM 15'-4"x15'-8"

LIVING ROOM 15'-4"x19'-8"

NO. 10028

60'-0"

Patio Contains Built-in Barbecue

No. 10064

Shake shingles, battened siding and natural stone are skillfully blended together to produce a beautiful facade for this home. The traffic pattern permits access to all rooms from the foyer without crossing another room. Sliding glass doors in the family room, dinette and master bedroom open onto the large patio-pool area. The built-in barbecue on the patio is roofed to provide a shaded area near the pool.

First floor — 2,585 sq. ft.
Basement — 2,585 sq. ft.
Garage — 493 sq. ft.

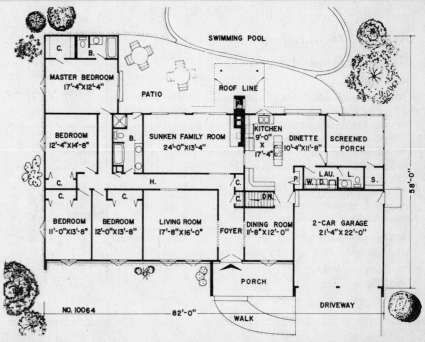

Firelight Enriches Living, Entertaining

No. 10136

Relaxed suburban living is the aim of this rambling traditional, highlighted by a striking three-way fireplace that lights and separates living and dining rooms. Expanses of sliding glass doors allow the area to share the terrace, and the corridor kitchen at right offers help in entertaining. Open to the kitchen is a useful complex which includes laundry, family room, and a closeted full bath near garage and basement work areas for ease of clean-up.

First floor — 1,888 sq. ft.
Basement — 1,184 sq. ft.
Garage — 590 sq. ft.

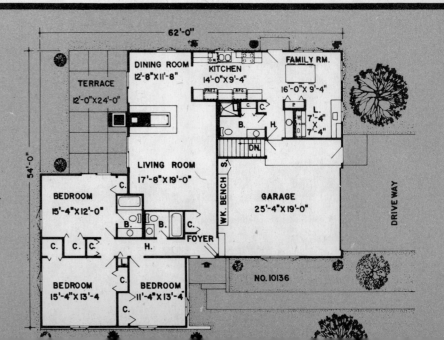

Angle Set for Entertaining, Relaxing

No. 10124

Striking and expensive, this three bedroom ranch style welcomes its angled plan as a means of effectively zoning living areas. To the left of the foyer, bedrooms are nestled around two full baths and are well-closeted for comfort. The bordering living room helps buffer noise and offers a quiet spot for relaxing. Entertaining is encouraged in the large, angular family room, which sports fireplace, bar, and sliding glass doors to the patio.

First floor — 2,180 sq. ft.
Basement — 2,042 sq. ft.
Garage and storage — 580 sq. ft.

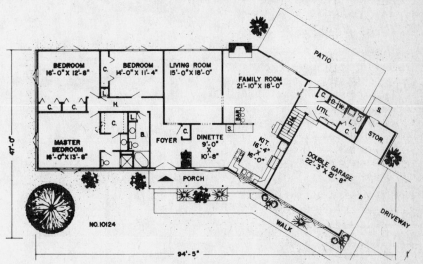

Central Atrium Highlights Well-organized Plan

No. 10464

Bring the outdoors in no matter what the season with glass-walled atrium incorporated into this elegant plan. The tiled family room carries out the indoor-outdoor living scheme and open room arrangement. The front living room has a large fireplace flanked with bookcases plus access to the dining room which is easily entered from the kitchen. A breakfast nook and convenient laundry area complete the functional areas of this home. Each of the spacious bedrooms has it own walk-in closet and bath. The master suite has a separate dressing room with five-piece bath.

**First floor — 2,222 sq. ft.
Garage — 468 sq. ft.**

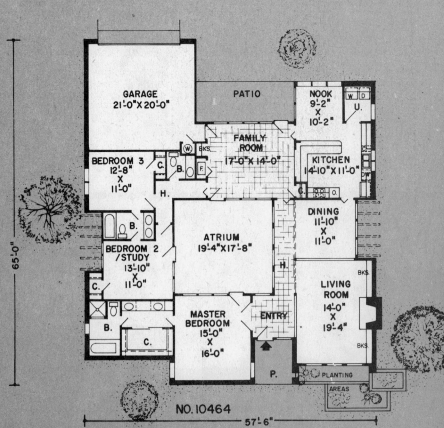

Multiple Wing Plan
Attired In Cut Stone

No. 9628

Spreading outward in three directions, this winged home is decked in vertical siding and trimmed in cupolas and cut stone. The gracious foyer admits guests to the living room or rear family room, both furnished with cut stone fireplaces. The master bedroom complex, equipped with a tub and shower bath as well as a dressing area, protrudes outward from the foyer and edges its own patio. Three more bedrooms and a bath flank the hall, which also connects to the rear terrace. A den situated behind the garage might adapt to an extra bedroom, sewing room, hobby shop, or office.

First floor — 2,716 sq. ft.
Basement — 1,568 sq. ft.
Garage — 493 sq. ft.

Simple Ranch Designates Living Zones

No. 246

With its three distinct living zones, this ranch is perfect for family living. The three bedrooms, including the master bedroom with its private bath, are separated from the living areas by a tile hallway that leads from the foyer to the living and family rooms. Well placed for entertaining, these two rooms plus the formal dining room comprise the central core of the home. A spacious terrace seems to expand the dining and family rooms because of the generous use of windows. Adjacent to the dining room is the U-shaped kitchen, complete with an area for informal family meals.

First floor — 1,642 sq. ft.
Garage — 462 sq. ft.

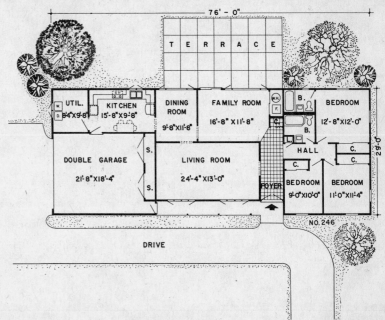

Airy Ranch Style Features Screen Patio

No. 10200

Open to the family room and steps from the kitchen for cookouts, the covered screened porch provides the perfect accent for this spacious and well-windowed contemporary ranch style. Central foyer and hallway channel traffic to bedrooms, formal living and dining rooms, and the expansive family room-kitchen complex. Serving as a focal point of the plan, the family-kitchen borders a utility room and shows entrances to back yard and garage. Three bedrooms and two full baths make up the sleeping wing.

First floor — 2,254 sq. ft.
Basement — 2,134 sq. ft.
Garage — 554 sq. ft.

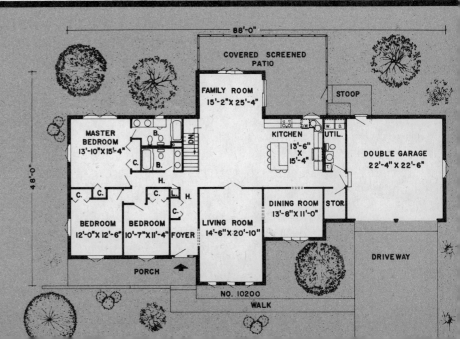

Living Room Highlights Ranch Style

No. 10176

Dramatically punctuated by a wood-burning fireplace on one end and glass access to the terrace on the other, the expansive living room becomes the focus of this distinctive ranch style. Two closets furnish the long foyer, and, to the right, three bedrooms and two full baths are nestled in the sleeping wing. Behind the double garage, the utility complex merits a laundry center and full bath with shower, while the large kitchen offers informal dining space.

First floor — 1,608 sq. ft.
Basement — 1,608 sq. ft.
Garage — 576 sq. ft.

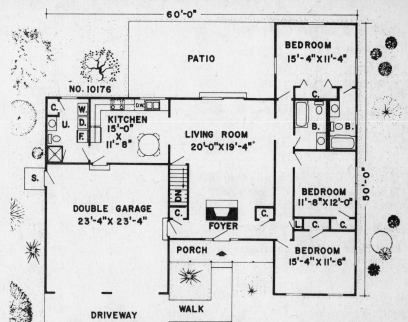

Spanish Styling Suits Narrow Lot

No. 10208

Elegant, elongated, and definitely Spanish in origin, this three bedroom home is accented with patios and designed to grace a narrow lot. Front entry garage borders an open patio with arched walkway which preludes entry into the home. Conveniently open to kitchen and family room, a covered patio is sandwiched between garage and living areas. Double closets line the foyer, which is flanked by living room and family room. Bedrooms are served by two full baths.

First floor — 1,600 sq. ft.
Basement — 1,600 sq. ft.
Garage — 586 sq. ft.

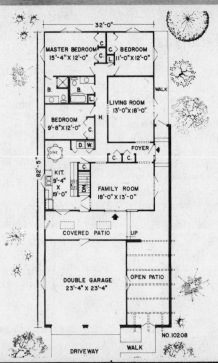

Design Focuses on Formality

No. 10214

Situated to overlook an impressive 27-ft. glassed-in porch, the dining room joins the formal living room of this ranch plan to create a workable unit for formal entertaining. A cozy fireplace furnishes the living room, and the large kitchen reserves space for family dining. Sizable and well-windowed, the master bedroom offers double closets, dressing area and full bath, and another full bath serves two more bedrooms. For convenience, the double garage opens directly into the foyer.

First floor — 1,651 sq. ft.
Basement — 1,651 sq. ft.
Garage — 521 sq. ft.

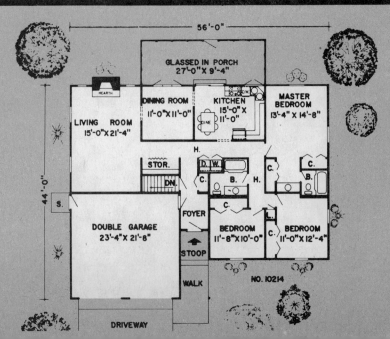

Porch Connects Garage, Foyer

No. 10212

Accessibility is a prime consideration in this trim three bedroom traditional, where the covered porch connects to the entry to provide shelter, a link to the garage, and warm welcome. Within steps of the foyer is a formal bow-windowed living room and a well-placed corridor kitchen. Laundry and half bath border the kitchen on one end, while an airy family room at the other end boasts a dining area, storage space, and sliding glass doors to the patio.

First floor — 2,055 sq. ft.
Basement — 2,055 sq. ft.
Garage — 522 sq. ft.

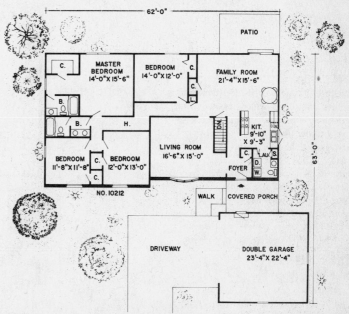

Airy Lattice Work Lends Charm to Central Core Design

No. 10453

The central traffic pattern for this unique design is the tiled foyer and hallway which links the dining room, living room and family room around a wet-bar that is accessible to all three rooms. Located at the far corner of the tiled hall are the kitchen, laundry and informal dining area. The step-saving arrangement of the kitchen is enhanced by the peninsula which links the area to the octagonal dining nook. The rear patio extends the open plan of the home as it is visible through the many windows located along the rear walls of the dining nook, the family room and the master bedroom.

First floor-2,115 sq. ft.
Garage-569 sq. ft.

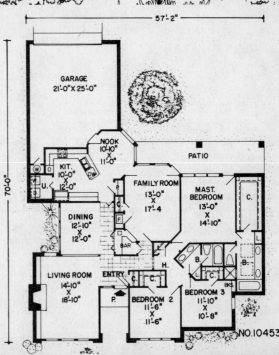

Tiled Hall Delineates Open Room Arrangement

No. 10463

From the glass-flanked entry a tiled walk-way leads around the perimeter of the central living areas and skirts the glass wall along the rear patio. The spacious family room includes an enclosed bar area which is also accessible from the living room. Interior windows separate the living room from the dining room which is just across the hall from the very functional kitchen. The bedrooms are located along the front of the home with the fourth bedroom well placed for a den or study. The master suite features a dressing room enhanced by a spacious whirlpool bath.

First floor - 2,410 sq. ft.
Garage - 614 sq. ft.

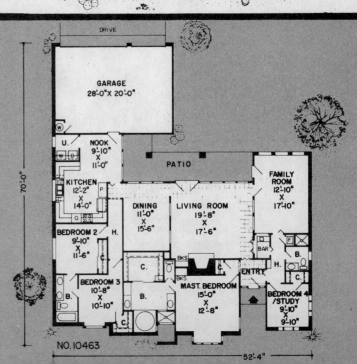

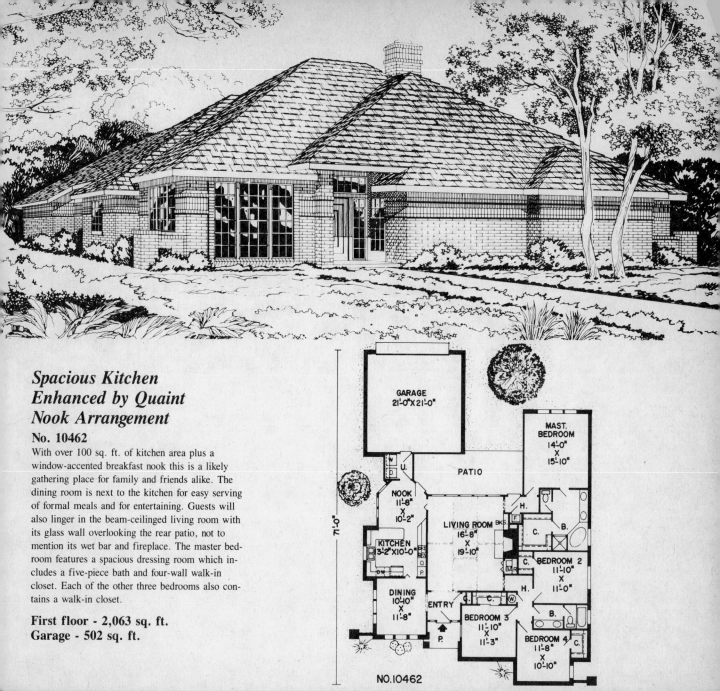

Spacious Kitchen
Enhanced by Quaint
Nook Arrangement

No. 10462

With over 100 sq. ft. of kitchen area plus a window-accented breakfast nook this is a likely gathering place for family and friends alike. The dining room is next to the kitchen for easy serving of formal meals and for entertaining. Guests will also linger in the beam-ceilinged living room with its glass wall overlooking the rear patio, not to mention its wet bar and fireplace. The master bedroom features a spacious dressing room which includes a five-piece bath and four-wall walk-in closet. Each of the other three bedrooms also contains a walk-in closet.

First floor - 2,063 sq. ft.
Garage - 502 sq. ft.

GARAGE
21'-0" X 21'-0"

MAST.
BEDROOM
14'-0"
X
15'-10"

PATIO

NOOK
11'-8"
X
10'-2"

LIVING ROOM
16'-8"
X
19'-10"

BEDROOM 2
11'-10"
X
11'-0"

KITCHEN
13'-2" X10'-0"

DINING
10'-10"
X
11'-8"

ENTRY

BEDROOM 3
11'-10"
X
11'-3"

BEDROOM 4
11'-8"
X
10'-10"

NO. 10462

Rugged Exterior
Characterizes Plan

No. 9264

Battened siding, shake shingles, and brick texture the exterior of this rustic ranch style, with its rugged beauty continued inside. Accessible from the foyer, the L-shaped living room and huge country kitchen dominate the living area and reinforce the illusion of wide open spaces. Wood-burning fireplace warms the living room, which opens to patio via sliding glass doors. Three bedrooms are nestled beyond the entry hall and spotlight the master bedroom with immense walk-in closet and full bath.

First floor — 1,744 sq. ft.
Basement — 1,744 sq. ft.
Garage — 499 sq. ft.

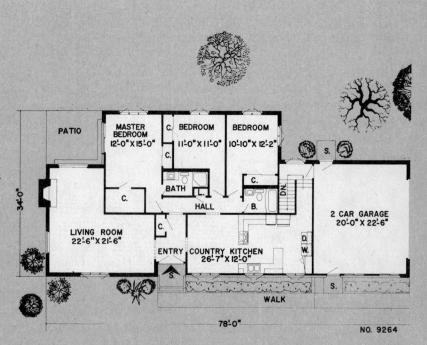

PATIO

MASTER BEDROOM
12'-0" X 15'-0"

C.

BEDROOM
11'-0" X 11'-0"

BEDROOM
10'-10" X 12'-2"

C.

C.

S.

34'-0"

C.

BATH

L.

C.

DN

2 CAR GARAGE
20'-0" X 22'-6"

HALL

B.

LIVING ROOM
22'-6" X 21'-6"

C.

ENTRY

COUNTRY KITCHEN
26'-7" X 12'-0"

D.
W.

S.

S.

WALK

78'-0"

NO. 9264

Novel Design Supplies
Sunny Interior

No. 9608

Shaped like a wedge of pie, this exceptional design offers individuality and an interior bathed in natural light. Overhead clerestory windows brighten the kitchen-family room, probably the central point of the home. Three large bedrooms and two full baths edge the left side, and the master bedroom boasts its own enclosed private patio. The rear terrace is reached not only through the family room but through a bedroom and bath as well. The formal living room which accommodates a fireplace, is set to the right of the foyer and another half bath for this area adjoins the family room.

First floor — 2,071 sq. ft.
Garage — 412 sq. ft.
Storage — 112 sq. ft.

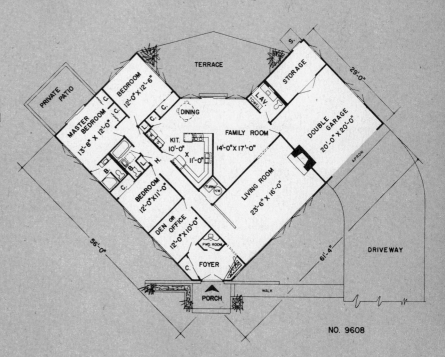

NO. 9608

Light, Bright Entry Hall

No. 10473

Good zoning and simplicity of construction make this house just right for an active, economy-minded family. The design can be adapted easily to a walkout basement with plenty of space available for a recreation room or more bedrooms. Family happenings and entertainment of guests center around the family room and the formal dining room. Each has convenient access to the spacious deck through sliding glass doors. The compact kitchen is open to the family room so the chef won't get lonely.

House – 1,632 sq. ft.

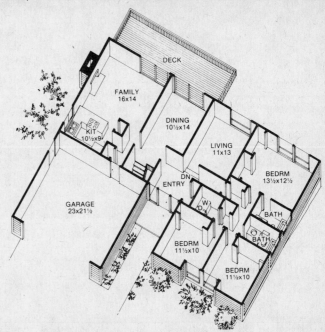

Unique Design Boasts Solarium

No. 21502

Tucked between the entry and the family room of this exceptional four bedroom plan, the solarium is the focal point of the home. Three baths are well placed, off the master bedroom, between the second and third bedrooms and near the fourth bedroom and family room. A spacious formal dining room and side entry garage are provided.

House – 2,270 sq. ft.
Garage – 473 sq. ft.

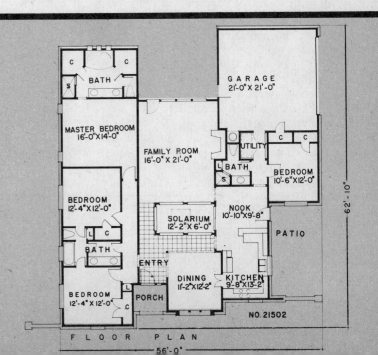

FLOOR PLAN

Patterned For Privacy

No. 10480

The exterior design of this home contributes to its privacy in subtle ways — the recessed windows, the roof overhang, the entryway niche. Only in back does the house open up to the outdoors. Yet there is plenty of natural light available in the front areas. The main entryway and the hallway from the garage to the living area are both conducive to growing all sorts of greenery. Family activity rooms — living/dining area and kitchen — are well away from the sleeping rooms. The main living/dining area is warmed by a fireplace and leads to a deck or patio in the backyard. A window in the efficiently designed U-shaped kitchen overlooks patio activities. The kitchen is compact and easy to maintain while providing three walls of counter space.

House – 1,665 sq. ft.

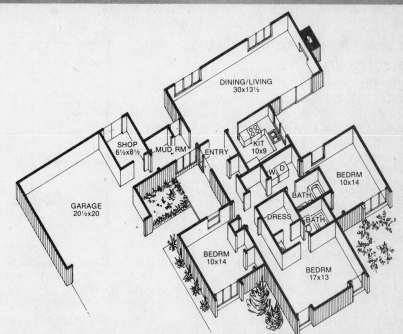

Contemporary Plan Styled for Activity

No. 334

Generously proportioned rooms, cathedral ceilings, and a sunken family room create an airy, spacious design that sets the mood for family activity. Built around convenience, this brick-trimmed contemporary calls for an open kitchen/dining area with snack bar and adjoining utility room for laundry chores. Three bedrooms and two full baths edge the plan, and the 20-foot living room is augmented by the large, vinyl-tiled family room, complete with sliding glass doors to the terrace.

First floor — 1,486 sq. ft.
Family room — 301 sq. ft.
Garage — 576 sq. ft.

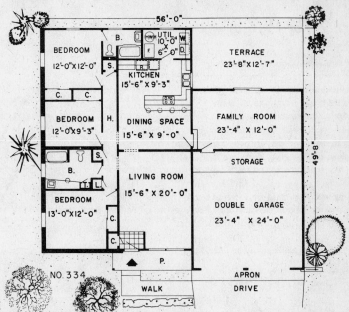

Barbecue Encourages Outdoor Living

No. 348

Entrance to this home is gained through a large foyer opening to a central hall. The large versatile living room/dining room area is centrally located between the kitchen and family room for maximum usage. Incorporated into the kitchen, itself is a breakfast area suitable for most of a busy family's meals.

First floor — 2,094 sq. ft.
Garage — 492 sq. ft.

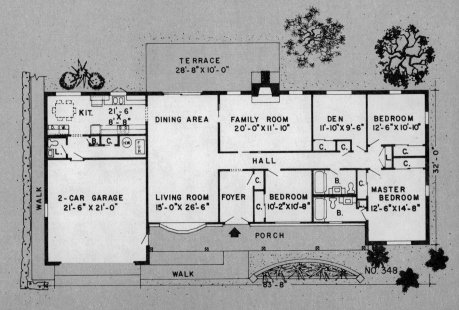

Private Patio Highlight Home

No. 342

Planned for convenience and livability, this four bedroom design offers an 18-foot patio, enclosed on three sides for maximum privacy. Adjoining family room and kitchen share a snack bar, and the combination mud room/laundry can be reached via garage, patio, or kitchen.

First floor — 1,869 sq. ft.
Basement — 1,703 sq. ft.
Garage — 546 sq. ft.

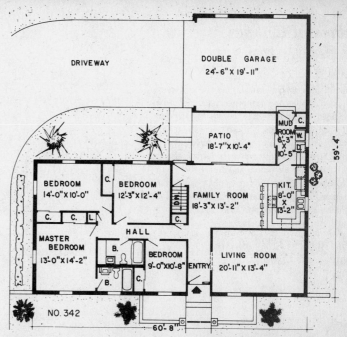

DRIVEWAY

DOUBLE GARAGE
24'-6" X 19'-11"

PATIO
18'-7" X 10'-4"

MUD ROOM
6'-3" X 10'-5"

C.

W.

D.

59'-4"

BEDROOM
14'-0" X 10'-0"

C.

BEDROOM
12'-3" X 12'-4"

FAMILY ROOM
18'-3" X 13'-2"

KIT.
8'-0" X 13'-2"

C.

MASTER BEDROOM
13'-0" X 14'-2"

HALL

B.

BEDROOM
9'-0" X 10'-8"

LIVING ROOM
20'-11" X 13'-4"

B.

C.

ENTRY

NO. 342

60'-8"

Cathedral Ceilings
Striking Decor

No. 9058

Visitors to this contemporary home are immediately struck by the awe-inspiring cathedral ceilings of the foyer, living and dining rooms and kitchen. The living room, recessed a foot below the foyer and dining room, has access to the terrace through sliding glass doors. Entrance to the terrace also is provided through the family and dining room. Three large bedrooms and two and one-half baths are planned to accommodate the large family, and the convenient mudroom provides laundry and closet space, plus a half-bath.

First floor — 1,970 sq. ft.
Garage — 526 sq. ft.

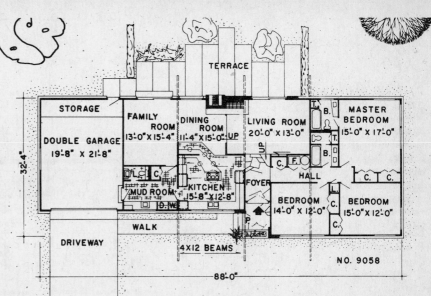

Screened Porch
Expands Dining Area

No. 9088

Skirting the open kitchen and dining area of this brick-sheathed design, the screened side porch presents an airy setting for family dining. A built-in barbecue serves the kitchen and family room, which also opens to a sprawling flagstone terrace. Bedrooms are sizable and baths efficient, especially the hall bath, an elongated double sink arrangement. Traffic is routed via the comfortable foyer and with coat closet, and the generous living and dining room savors a wood-burning fireplace.

First floor — 1,776 sq. ft.
Basement — 1,776 sq. ft.

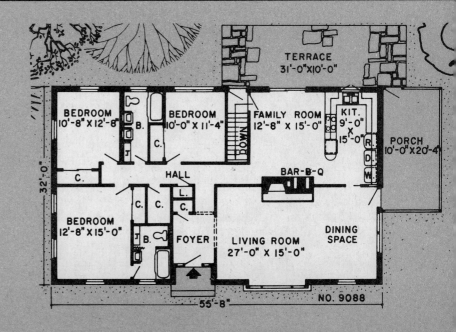

Family Room Nucleus of Ranch Plan

No. 9060

Sliding glass doors admit light and involve indoors with outdoors in the centrally located family room of this sleek ranch style. Placed to invite access from living and sleeping areas, the family room provides informal contrast to the living room, isolated and free from traffic. Tucked between family room and garage, the compact U-shaped kitchen is placed for easy transportation of groceries and has access to basement stairway. Three bedrooms include an ample master bedroom favored with double closets and compartmented bath.

First floor — 1,609 sq. ft.
Basement — 1,609 sq. ft.
Garage — 572 sq. ft.

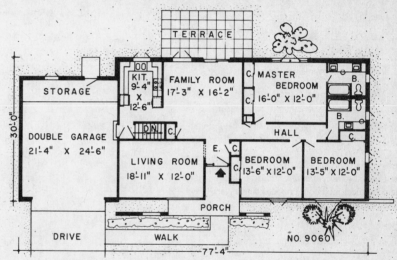

Single-Level Contemporary

No. 10402

Vertical board and brick sliding blend together to give attractiveness to the exterior of this one-story contemporary home. Inside are featured three bedrooms with large closets, two and one-half baths, a kitchen which lies centralized between the family and living rooms and a full basement. The two car garage is entered from the side.

**First floor-1,764 sq. ft.
Basement-1,764 sq. ft.
Garage-435 sq. ft.**

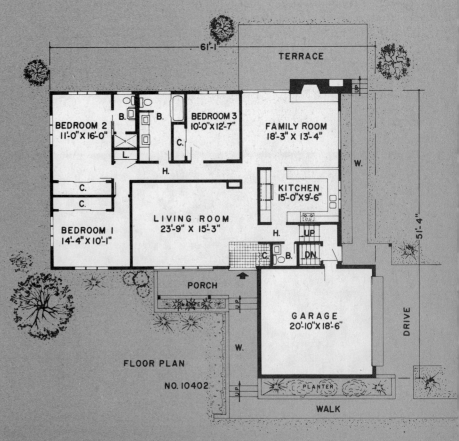

Traffic Patterns Carefully Designed

No. 10410

Careful thought has been given to traffic patterns in this single-level which funnels movements along hallways rather than through rooms. Family diners may assemble in the nook, family room, or terrace, depending on the season and occasion. A 6 × 1 opening from kitchen to family room makes passage of food and dishes handy, and access from kitchen to terrace encourages convenient barbequing. Notice the generous amount of storage; large closets in each of the three bedrooms, built-in cabinets flanking family room raised hearth fireplace, kitchen broom closet, and large storage area in double carport.

First floor — 1,621 sq. ft.
Garage — 435 sq. ft.

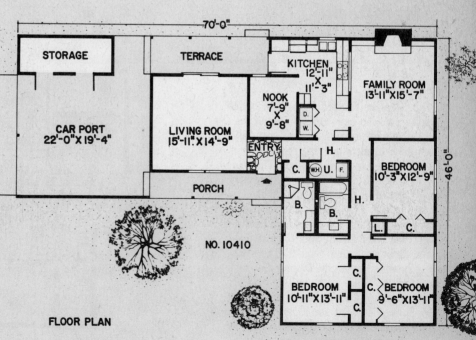

FLOOR PLAN

Magnificent
Living Room
Defines Core of Home

No. 10448

The fireplace flanked by built-in bookcases plus the beamed ceiling and the window wall overlooking the rear patio combine to form a living room that invites family and guests alike. The more informal area of the house incorporates the glassed-in breakfast nook with its own private patio, the capacious pantry and the efficient kitchen which opens onto the large family room across a comfortable serving counter. The sleeping quarters are located along the right side of the house with the two smaller bedrooms toward the front and the master suite occupying the more secluded rear area. The dressing room within the suite is illuminated by a skylight.

First floor-2,361 sq. ft.
Garage-509 sq. ft.

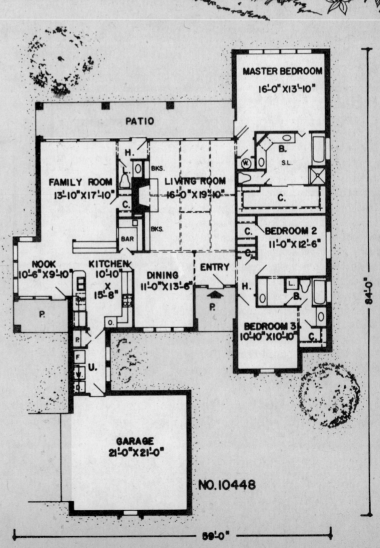

Central Living Area Invites Entertaining

No. 10449

With a wetbar that can be accessed from either the family room or the living room plus the dining room's location just off the entry, this easy-living arrangement provides plenty of room for parties or holiday open houses. Food preparation is a breeze in the roomy kitchen that incorporates plenty of storage space and an angled peninsula which organizes the space into work areas and informal dining. Luxurious appointments can be seen in the bedrooms of this home. Each of the two smaller bedrooms has a private vanity area which adjoins the shared bathing area. The master suite has walk-in closets and a five piece bath.

First floor-2,270 sq. ft.
Garage-493 sq. ft.

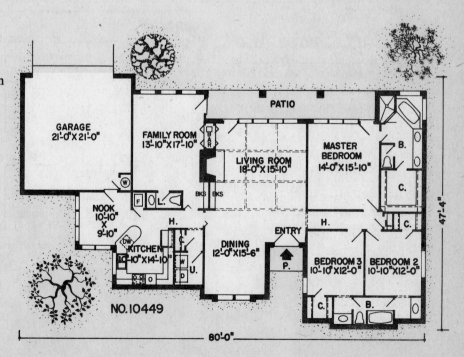

GARAGE 21'-0" X 21'-0"

FAMILY ROOM 13'-10" X 17'-10"

PATIO

LIVING ROOM 18'-0" X 15'-10"

MASTER BEDROOM 14'-0" X 15'-10"

NOOK 10'-10" X 9'-10"

KITCHEN 10'-10" X 14'-10"

DINING 12'-0" X 15'-6"

ENTRY

BEDROOM 3 10'-10" X 12'-0"

BEDROOM 2 10'-10" X 12'-0"

NO. 10449

60'-0"

47'-4"

Skylights, Space Mark Contemporary Plan

No. 10298

Natural light from skylights floods this three bedroom contemporary, a well-designed home that focuses on space. Rooms are airy and include a 19-ft. family room that annexes a patio, a 12-ft. dinning area, and an 18-ft. living room with wood-burning fireplace. Master bedroom is favored with a separate dressing room and private bath.

First floor — 1,889 sq. ft.
Garage — 491 sq. ft.
Basement — 1,889 sq. ft.

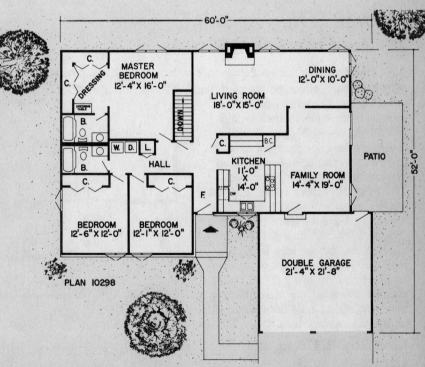

PLAN 10298

60'-0"
52'-0"

MASTER BEDROOM 12'-4" X 16'-0"
DRESSING
DRESSING TABLE
B.
W. D. L.
B.
HALL
BEDROOM 12'-6" X 12'-0"
BEDROOM 12'-1" X 12'-0"
DOWN
LIVING ROOM 18'-0" X 15'-0"
DINING 12'-0" X 10'-0"
C.
B.C.
KITCHEN 11'-0" X 14'-0"
DW
FAMILY ROOM 14'-4" X 19'-0"
PATIO
F.
DOUBLE GARAGE 21'-4" X 21'-8"

Activity Wings Define Ranch Plan

No. 10318

Three wings effectively separate sleeping areas, activity areas, and garage in this three bedroom ranch style. In the sleeping wing, large bedrooms are grouped with baths and sewing room, while the main wing offers formal living and dining rooms backed by kitchen and activities room. Two patios are featured.

First floor — 2,082 sq. ft.
Garage — 583 sq. ft.
Basement — 1,008 sq. ft.

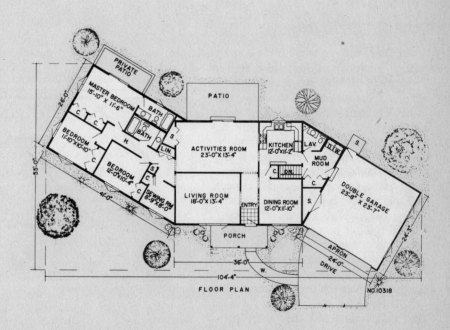

FLOOR PLAN

Two Story Underground

No. 10416

Many energy-wise features have been incorporated into this two-story underground, best suited for a southern exposure. The sunroom on lower level shows a 4″ concrete floor and can be entered from either the utility room or front bedroom. Three plastic roof panels allow an abudance of sunshine to warm this space. Living room, which is raised 8″, and family room each have a circulating fireplace, sharing one chimney. Brick from the rear of the living room fireplace extends into the dining room, flanked on either side by shelves, and open above the shelves to encourage air circulation between the two rooms. With ample space for washer, dryer, furnace, hot water heater, sink and vanity, the utility room lies conveniently close just below the kitchen.

Lower level — 1,441 sq. ft.
Main level — 1,986 sq. ft.
Workshop & Hall — 292 sq. ft.
Garage — 588 sq. ft.

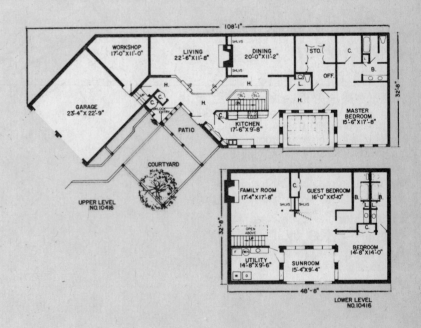

Screened Porch
Extends Dining Area

No. 10266

Outdoor living areas are spotlighted in this one level plan, where the living room overlooks a private garden, the family room opens to a patio, and the dining area is enlarged by the adjacent screened porch. Also exceptional is the kitchen complex, which offers planning desk, dining area, and pantry and borders a laundry/half bath. Three bedrooms are outlined.

First floor — 1,807 sq. ft.
Basement — 1,807 sq. ft.
Porch — 160 sq. ft.
Garage — 539 sq. ft.

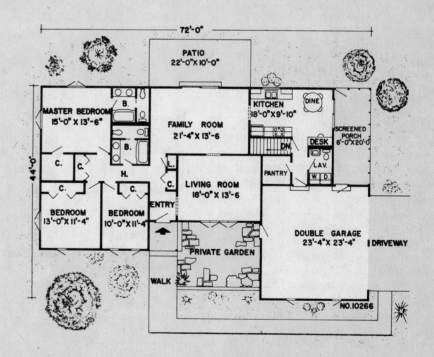

Three Fireplaces Included

No. 10406

An attractive mixture of brick and bevel siding gives this single-story ranch character while the wood shingle roof not only adds to its value, but increases its good looks also. Basement space could include a fireplaced recreation room and expanses of storage. Two additional fireplaces grace the family room and sunken living room. Although no formal dining area is provided for, the 20 × 12 family room allows ample space for eating facilities. Two full baths and three bedrooms, including a sunny corner bedroom, comprise a secluded sleeping wing. Situated near three entrances, the laundry room and adjacent bath with shower make a perfect mud room combination.

First floor — 732 sq. ft.
Basement — 1, 496 sq. ft.
Garage — 463 sq. ft.

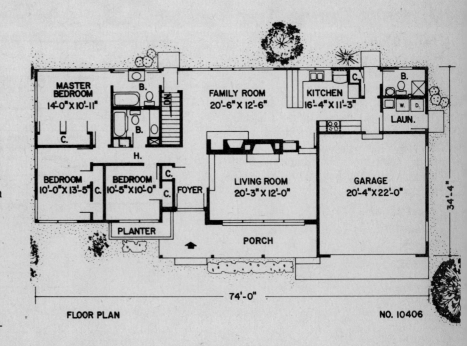

FLOOR PLAN   NO. 10406

Energy Saving Options

No. 10424

Varied living patterns are neatly divided, locating the home's three bedrooms on the left side, and busier areas on the right. The dining room is set off from the living room by a lowered ceiling and stately brick pillar. A bar tucks away behind folding doors on one side of the living room's raised hearth fireplace, and built-in bookshelves on the other. Wise architectural planning allows for energy consciousness by the homeowner. Bi-folding doors make it possible to shut off and not heat almost any section of the home. Expanses of glass are located in both the front and rear, adding natural light to the design, giving and excellent view and allowing the sun's warmth to bathe living areas.

First floor — 1,800 sq. ft.
Garage — 503 sq. ft.
Patio & Porch — 283 sq. ft.

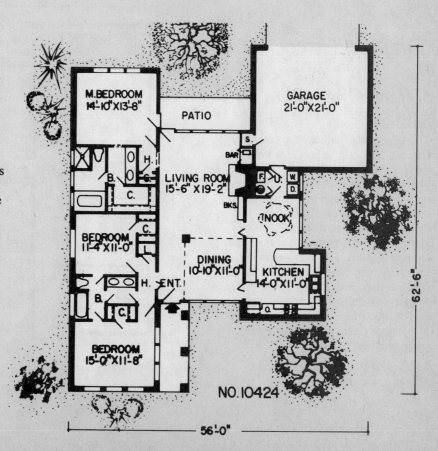

M. BEDROOM
14'-10" X 13'-8"

PATIO

GARAGE
21'-0" X 21'-0"

BAR

LIVING ROOM
15'-6" X 19'-2"

BKS.

NOOK

BEDROOM
11'-4" X 11'-0"

DINING
10'-10" X 11'-0"

KITCHEN
14'-0" X 11'-0"

ENT.

BEDROOM
15'-0" X 11'-8"

NO. 10424

62'-6"

56'-0"

Compact Three-bedroom Design Offers Open Plan

No. 10487

The large great room with its massive fireplace and easy access to a lovely patio is the center of this inviting design. The informal, yet efficient kitchen opens onto the family room and is just next to the formal dining area. The three bedrooms are arranged along the opposite side of the home with the spacious master suite separated from the front bedrooms by two baths. A full-wall closet plus a roomy dressing area yield plenty of space for the busy, working couple. Each of the front bedrooms has an ample walk-in closet plus a shared, compartmentalized bath.

First floor — 1,611 sq. ft.
Garage — 486 sq. ft.

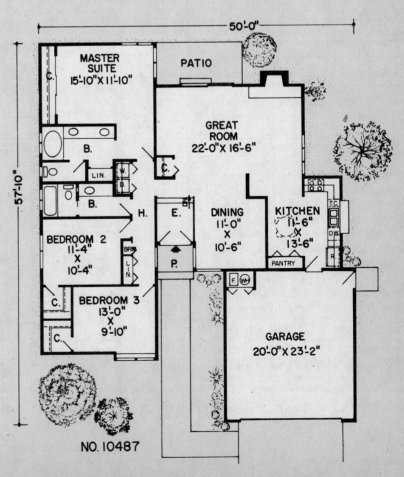

NO. 10487

Active/Passive Combination

No. 10372

The exterior appearance of this house readily draws your attention to its passive and active solar systems. Features include large triple glazed south windows, solar roof panels and a trombe thermal wall which receives heat gain from the sun to radiate into the room on cloudy days or at night. Heat gain is also obtained from clerestory windows which shed the sun's rays on solid brick north walls. A six inch concrete floor is employed for heat gain and storage. An open family room forms the focus of the floor plan. A formal living room, three bedrooms, two baths and a utility room are more secluded. The family room flows into the bright south-facing kitchen through a dining bar window. A double garage sits at the rear and is reached through a side entrance. Varied roof pitches give height to the single-level design.

Living area — 1,787 sq. ft.
Basement — 650 sq. ft.
Garage — 576 sq. ft.

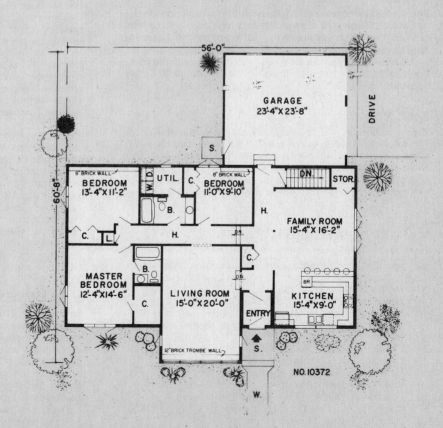

Order Your New Home

GARLINGHOUSE

Materials List Available with Most Home Plans

From a Company With Over 75 Years Of Experience.

GET RESULTS FAST!

Your Garlinghouse blueprints will speed the construction of your new home. For over 75 years, our homes have been built by tens of thousands of families across the nation and around the world. You can use our plans with confidence. Every detail of construction is already worked out for you. Our complete, accurate blueprints contain all the information a builder needs to begin construction, NOW!

SAVE MONEY

There's no cheaper way to have the home you've always wanted. The costs of designing our unique homes are spread out over a number of home plan buyers nationwide. You pay only a fraction of what you would spend to have a home designed for you by a high-priced architect or professional designer. And, our years of experience help you avoid costly mistakes and delays during construction.

YOU GET EVERYTHING YOU NEED

Every set of Garlinghouse blueprints contains:
1) Four Elevations (front drawn ¼" scale, other sides drawn ⅛" scale)
2) Floor Plans (for all floors)
3) Basement and/or Foundation Plan
4) Roof Plan (drawn ⅛" scale)
5) Typical Wall Sections (cross sectional slices through the home)
6) Kitchen and Bath Cabinet Details
7) Fireplace Detail (where applicable)
8) Details for Stairs (where applicable)
9) Plot Plan (drawn ⅛" scale)
10) Location of Electrical Fixtures and Components
11) Complete Materials List (only if ordered)
12) Specifications and Contract Form
13) Energy Conservation Specifications Guide

(NOTE: all drawings are made ¼" to 1" scale or larger, except as noted above)

DO YOU NEED A MATERIALS LIST?

We recommend that you get one. Experience shows that it saves you time and money. This list gives the dimensions and specifications of all materials needed to build your home, except for small hardware (like nails and screws) and the air conditioning, electrical and plumbing materials (these vary depending upon your local building codes). With the materials list, you'll get faster, more accurate bids and speed every step of the construction of your home.

BLUEPRINT MODIFICATIONS LET YOU ADD A PERSONAL TOUCH

Your home doesn't have to be a look-a-like. Design modifications can be made allowing you to customize our home plan to your own special needs. Minor non-structural changes and building material substitutions can be made by any competent builder without the need for expensive blueprint revisions.

However, if you are considering making major changes to your design, then we strongly recommend that you seek the services of an architect or professional designer to assist you. Even these expensive professional services will cost less with our complete, detailed plans as a starting point.

The Garlinghouse Design Staff is always available to help you. We can assist you with your new home project and can make any alterations to your design that you wish for a very reasonable hourly charge. The advantage of working with us is that we'll make your design modifications directly to our original drawings. We'll provide you with a new, complete set of blueprints to your exact specifications. Other architects or professional designers can only attach modified drawings to our original blueprints. This approach is more confusing, often more time consuming, and may lead to expensive mistakes or delays. Call us for further information on our inexpensive design modification services.

HOW MANY SETS OF PLANS WILL YOU NEED?

We recommend that you purchase eight sets of blueprints. Once you begin the process of building your home, everyone seems to need a set. Your lending institution (1) and local building authority (2) each need a set. And, of course, your general building contractor (3) will need one. Then, all of his subcontractors will need a set . . . the foundation contractor (4), the framing carpenter (5), the plumbing contractor (6), the heating and air conditioning contractor (7), the electrical contractor (8), the insulation contractor, drywall contractor, finish carpenter, etc. While some sets can be shared, or handed along as work progresses, experience shows that you'll get faster, cheaper, and better results with the standard 8-set package.

Blueprints Today

REVERSE PLANS

You may find that a particular house would suit your taste or your lot conditions better if it were reversed. A reverse plan turns the design end-over-end. That is, if the garage is shown on the left side and the bedrooms on the right, the reverse plan will show the garage on the right side and the bedrooms on the left. To see quickly how a design will look in reverse, hold the book in front of a mirror.

The dimensions and lettering in many Garlinghouse reverse plans are corrected to be right reading. When this is not the case, one mirror-image, reversed set is produced for reference by you and your builder. The rest are then sent "as shown", for ease in reading the lettering and dimensions, and marked with a special "Reversed" stamp to eliminate confusion. (Available only on multiple set orders.)

PRICE SCHEDULE

One Complete Set of Blueprints	$95.00
Minimum Construction Package (5 sets)	$135.00
Standard Construction Package (8 sets)	$160.00
Each Additional Set Ordered With One of the Above Packages	$20.00
Materials List to be Included With Each Set of Blueprints Ordered	$15.00

PRICES ARE SUBJECT TO CHANGE WITHOUT NOTICE

WHEN WILL YOU RECEIVE YOUR ORDER?

We process and ship your order within 48 hours of receipt. Then, it usually takes another 5 to 7 days for delivery. Please allow 10 full working days for delivery from the time we receive your order. For fastest service, use your Visa or MasterCard and call our toll free telephone number.

If you are in a big hurry for your order, we offer ultra-fast Federal Express delivery service. If you call in your order before 12:00 noon (Central Time), then we can provide guaranteed next day delivery to anywhere in the U.S. for a mailing charge of $40.00 ($50.00 for Alaska, Hawaii or Puerto Rico). Guaranteed second day delivery is available for only $18.00 ($28.00 for Alaska, Hawaii or Puerto Rico).

INTERNATIONAL ORDERS

If you are ordering from outside the United States, then your check, money order, or international money transfer must be **payable in U.S. currency.**

Because of extremely long delays involved with surface mail, we ship all international orders via Air Parcel Post. Please refer to the schedule below for mailing charges on these orders:

COUNTRY	ONE SET	MULTIPLE SETS
Canada	$ 5.75	$ 9.75
Mexico & Carribean Nations	$ 9.00	$16.00
All Other Nations	$12.50	$24.75

IMPORTANT

Whenever possible, blueprint orders are shipped UPS for fast delivery. Therefore, please include your complete street address (rather than a post office box number). If you use a rural route delivery box, then a street location is also helpful. If no one is at home during the day, then you might want to give your work address to ensure proper delivery.

BLUEPRINT ORDER FORM   07021

PLEASE SEND ME
- ☐ One Complete Set of Blueprints ($95.00)
- ☐ Minimum Construction Package: five sets ($135.00)
- ☐ Standard Construction Package: eight sets ($160.00)

Plan Number _____ ☐ as shown   ☐ reversed

Cost . . . . $_____

____ Additional Set(s) $20.00 each . . . . $_____

Materials List ($15.00 per order) . . . . $_____

Mailing Charges . . . . $___4.25___

TOTAL AMOUNT ENCLOSED . . . . $_____

(Kansas residents add 4%)

Purchaser hereby agrees that the home plan construction drawings being purchased will not be used for the construction of more than one single dwelling, and that these drawings will not be reproduced, either in whole or in part, by any means whatsoever.

CHARGE MY ORDER TO: ☐ MasterCard   ☐ Visa

Card # |_|_|_|_|_|_|_|_|_|_|_|_|_|_|_|_|

Exp. Date _____ Signature _____

Name _____

Address _____

City & State _____ Zip _____

Daytime Telephone Number _____

The Garlinghouse Co., 320 S.W. 33rd St., P.O. Box 299
(913) 267-2490   Topeka, Kansas 66601-0299

BLUEPRINT ORDER FORM   07021

PLEASE SEND ME
- ☐ One Complete Set of Blueprints ($95.00)
- ☐ Minimum Construction Package: five sets ($135.00)
- ☐ Standard Construction Package: eight sets ($160.00)

Plan Number _____ ☐ as shown   ☐ reversed

Cost . . . . $_____

____ Additional Set(s) $20.00 each . . . . $_____

Materials List ($15.00 per order) . . . . $_____

Mailing Charges . . . . $___4.25___

TOTAL AMOUNT ENCLOSED . . . . $_____

(Kansas residents add 4%)

Purchaser hereby agrees that the home plan construction drawings being purchased will not be used for the construction of more than one single dwelling, and that these drawings will not be reproduced, either in whole or in part, by any means whatsoever.

CHARGE MY ORDER TO: ☐ MasterCard   ☐ Visa

Card # |_|_|_|_|_|_|_|_|_|_|_|_|_|_|_|_|

Exp. Date _____ Signature _____

Name _____

Address _____

City & State _____ Zip _____

Daytime Telephone Number _____

The Garlinghouse Co., 320 S.W. 33rd St., P.O. Box 299
(913) 267-2490   Topeka, Kansas 66601-0299

Building Books

The books on this page were written with the professional home builder in mind. They are all comprehensive information sources for contractors or for those beginners who wish to build like contractors.

2546. Blueprint Reading For Construction This combination text and workbook shows and tells how to read residential, commercial, and light industrial prints. With an abundance of actual drawings from industry, you learn step by step about each component of a set of blueprints, including even cost estimating. 336 pp.; Goodheart-Wilcox (spiral bound) $25.20

2516. Building Consultant The new home buyer's bible to home construction. This encyclopedia of home building explains in comprehensive detail about all the various elements that go into a completed house. It enables you to deal with the construction of your new home in a meaningful way that will avoid costly errors, whether you use a contractor or build it yourself. 188 pp.; Holland House (paperback) $8.95

2570. Modern Masonry Everything you will ever need to know about concrete, masonry and brick is included in this book. Forms construction, concrete reinforcement, proper foundation construction, and bricklaying are among the topics covered in step-by-step detail. An excellent all-round reference and guide. 256 pp.; 700 illus. Goodheart-Willcox $14.64

2504. Architecture, Residential Drawing and Design An excellent text that explains all the fundamentals on how to create a complete set of construction drawings. Specific areas covered include proper design and planning considerations, foundation plans, floor plans, elevations, stairway details, electrical plans, plumbing plans, etc. 492 pp.; over 800 illus. Goodheart-Willcox $29.10

2508. Modern Plumbing All aspects of plumbing installation, service, and repair are presented here in illustrated, easy-to-follow text. This book contains all the information needed for vocational competence, including the most up-to-date tools, materials, and practices. 300 pp.; over 700 illus. Goodheart-Willcox $16.00

2506. House Wiring Simplified This book teaches all the fundamentals of modern house wiring; shows how it's done with easy-to-understand drawings. A thorough guide to the materials and practices for safe, efficient installation of home electrical systems. 176 pp.; 384 illus. Goodheart-Willcox $8.80

2510. Modern Carpentry A complete guide to the "nuts and bolts" of building a home. This book explains all about building materials, framing, trim work, insulation, foundations, and much more. A valuable text and reference guide. 492 pp.; over 1400 illus. Goodheart-Willcox $19.40

2544. Solar Houses An examination of solar homes from the standpoint of lifestyle. This publication shows you through photographs, interviews, and practical information, what a solar lifestyle involves, how owners react to it, and what the bottom-line economics are. Included are 130 floor plans and diagrams which give you a clear idea of how various "active" and "passive" solar systems work. 160 pp.; 370, illus. Pantheon (paperback) **$9.95**

2586. How to Design & Remodel Kitchens — This book takes you through steps beginning with evaluating your present kitchen and designing a new one to hiring a contractor or doing the work yourself. It offers solid information on the things you need to know to create the kitchen that best fits your needs. Full color charts and illustrations. 96 pp.; Ortho (paperback) **$5.95**

2588. How to Design & Remodel Bathrooms — This helpful guide shows you step-by-step procedures for designing or remodeling your bathrooms so they suit the needs of your family. Clear charts, illustrations and text present information and techniques necessary for undertaking this immense project. Full color, 96 pp.; Ortho (paperback) **$5.95**

2518. Build Your Own Home An authoritative guide on how to be your own general contractor. This book goes through the step-by-step process of building a house with special emphasis on the business aspects such as financing, scheduling, permits, insurance, and more. Furthermore, it gives you an understanding of what to expect out of your various subcontractors so that you can properly orchestrate their work. 106 pp.; Holland House (paperback) **$8.95**

2572. Super Insulated Houses — A superinsulated house is one which is so well-insulated and air tight that nearly all necessary heat is supplied by passive solar energy, electric lights and appliances, human bodies, etc. A superinsulated house requires less than 15% of the auxiliary energy needed for a pre-1974 house. This construction technique means big energy savings to the home owner, and this book is by far the most complete analysis of superinsulated houses to date. 112 pp.; Brick House (paperback) **$7.95**

2554. Underground Houses A fabulously detailed account of the actual building process for an underground home. This book follows the author through the step-by-step construction of his 910 square foot energy efficient, sub-grade dwelling (which incidentally cost only $6,750 to build). If you are interested in building an underground home with your own two hands and you want to build it right the first time, then you will want to have this well illustrated, easy to follow guide. 128 pp.; Sterling (paperback) **$6.95**

2576. Home Wind Power—Originally published by the U.S. Department of Energy under the title "Wind Power for Farms, Homes and Small Industry," this manuscript is by far the most comprehensive and easy to understand, dealing with this subject, on the market, today. Everything you need to know to install your own wind energy system is included in this book. Average wind power distribution in the U.S. and Canada; wind power variations with height and local terrain; possible legal hurdles including wind rights; insurance liabilities and warranties; sharing, buying and selling power; are just a few of the many topics dealt with in this extraordinary publication. 208 pp.; Garden Way (paperback) **$10.95**

2560. The House Book How livable your new home turns out to be is determined primarily by the interior finishing and decorating that goes into your home. This book is the bible of home decorating, covering absolutely every aspect of interior finishing. It contains over 1,000 color photographs with a wealth of ideas new to the U.S. (European decors). This is the most comprehensive and informative book on home decorating that you can buy. It's well worth the investment. 448 pp.; Crown (paperback) **$14.95**

2592. How to Design & Build Decks & Patios — Learn how to create decks and patios to suit every type of lot and lifestyle. This fully illustrated source book includes detailed information on design and construction as well as special charts on building and paving materials. Full color, 112 pp.; Ortho (paperback) **$5.95**

2514. The Underground House Book For anyone seriously interested in building and living in an underground home, this book tells it all. Aesthetic considerations, building codes, site planning, financing, insurance, planning and decorating considerations, maintenance costs, soil, excavation, landscaping, water considerations, humidity control, and specific case histories are among the many facets of underground living dealt with in this publication. 208 pp.; 140 illus. Garden Way **$10.95**

2562. How To Design and Build Your Own House Illustrated with almost 700 drawings (every step of the way), this complete do-it-yourself manual enables you, the beginner, to design and construct your own house. From putting together your first ideas and translating them into working drawings to figuring out costs and the actual construction of the house. The most complete and best illustrated book on the subject. 384 pp.; Alfred A. Knopf (paperback) **$11.95**

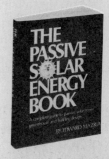

2540. The Passive Solar Energy Book A surprisingly complete guide to passive solar home, greenhouse, and building design. This book presents a step-by-step process for choosing and sizing the systems best suited for your particular needs. Includes information about solar radiation, regional climate variations, and space heat losses and gains so that you can calculate heating/cooling requirements and determine the potential money savings with a passive solar system. 448 pp.; 238 illus. Rodale (paperback) **$14.95**

Building Books Order Form

PLEASE SEND ME THE FOLLOWING BOOKS:

Book Order Number	Price
_____	$ _____
_____	$ _____
_____	$ _____
_____	$ _____
_____	$ _____
Postage and Handling	$ _____1.75_____
Add 50¢ For Each Additional Book	$ _____
Kansas Residents Add 4% Sales Tax	$ _____
TOTAL ENCLOSED	**$** _____

- Orders usually shipped the same day they are received
- International Orders include an additional $1.50 per book for surface mail

CHARGE MY ORDER TO:

☐ **MasterCard**   ☐ **Visa**

Card # _____

Exp. Date _____

Signature _____

_____

MY SHIPPING ADDRESS IS:
(Please Print)

Name _____

Address _____

City _____

State _____ Zip _____

SEND ORDER TO: 07020

The Garlinghouse Company
P.O. Box 299
Topeka, Kansas 66601-0299

2590. All About Landscaping — Beautifully landscaped property adds to the enjoyment of your home and yard and increases the value of your house. This well-illustrated guide includes the techniques, tools and insights you need to create a landscape that is uniquely your own. Covers all aspects from design through construction. Full color, 96 pp.; Ortho (paperback) **$5.95**

2542. Designing and Building A Solar House Written by one of America's foremost authorities on solar architecture. It is a practical "how-to" guide that clearly demonstrates the most sensible ways to marry good house design with contemporary solar technology. Included is a thorough discussion of both "active" and "passive" solar systems, and even a listing of the today's leading solar homes. 288 pp.; 400 illus. Garden Way (paperback) **$10.95**

2650. Multi-level Hillside & Solar Home Plans

2652. Traditional Home Plans

2654. Small Home Plans

2655. Vacation & Leisure Home Plans

Each of these five books contains over 120 new, innovative home designs from the finest architects and designers all over America. Many full color illustrations, and blueprints are available for all homes. 116 pp.; Garlinghouse (paperback). Each **$2.50**

2671. Project Plans to Build for Children

2672. Project Plans for All Around the House

2673. Project Plans for Outdoor Living

These idea-packed books contain the most extensive collections of Better Homes & Gardens project plans ever published in a single book or magazine. Each book contains over 125 plans plus full color or black and white photographs of finished projects, diagrams and instructions. In addition to the instructions included in the books, there are order forms for working blueprints and materials lists for selected projects. The three books complement one another and offer many additional ideas for decorating or for future reference when adding on or remodeling. 128 pp.; Garlinghouse (paperback). Each **$3.95**